DAILY WORD

WITH JENNIFER

DAILY WORD WITH JENNIFER

JENNIFER DUNN COOLEY

For speaking inquires, permissions requests, and general questions contact the author by visiting dailywordwithjennifer.com

Printed in the United States of America.
First paperback edition June 2022.

Cover and layout design by G Sharp Design, LLC.
www.gsharpmajor.com

Front cover and back cover photos by Misty Webb, M&D Images.
www.m-dimages.com

ISBN 979-8-836-43291-1 (paperback)

Dear Reader:

Thank you for your purchase of this devotional! I pray that you will find encouragement and hope as you read each devotional entry on a daily basis. This devotional was inspired from the **dailywordwithjennifer.com** blog and has taken almost three years to complete. Please be patient with me as a first-time author and know that my heart sincerely desires to encourage you on your faith journey.

> "So let us encourage one another and build each other up, just as you are already doing."
>
> **1 THESSALONIANS 5:11**

God bless you,

Jennifer

JANUARY

"For I know the plans I have for you," says the Lord. "They are plans for good and not for disaster, to give you a future and a hope. In those days when you pray, I will listen."

Jeremiah 29:11-12

January 1

> "For I know the plans I have for you," says the Lord. "They are plans for good and not for disaster, to give you a future and a hope. In those days when you pray, I will listen."
>
> **JEREMIAH 29:11-12**

What does this scripture mean to you? I can tell you that there have been times this particular scripture has placed a smile on my face even when my heart was heavy. To know that God has a plan for my life is to know that HE must have created each one of us for a specific purpose. And if you continue with that same thought process, it would be completely illogical to think HE would cause us harm since HE created/designed us for a purpose. When I hear people talk negatively about God not loving them, God being constantly mad with them, or God causing bad things to happen to them, I think that is the OPPOSITE of God. He is our Creator. He designed each one of us for a unique purpose. He called us by name. He cherishes us. And He desires fellowship with us.

Prayer is talking to God. Use this time right now to say hello to Him, tell Him about your thoughts, dreams, concerns, and let Him remind you that He has a good plan for your life.

Jennifer

Prayer Request

January 2

> "And no one puts new wine into old wineskins. For the old skins would burst from the pressure, spilling the wine and ruining the skins. New wine is stored in new wineskins so that both are preserved."
>
> **MATTHEW 9:17**

Notice that old wineskins had limitations on what they could successfully store for their owner. If the owner attempted to place new wine into the old wineskins, the wineskins would burst, which ruined the storage device (wineskins) AND the valuable wine. What a terrible waste!

As you step into this new year, what "old wineskins" are you carrying around with you? What former limitations/restrictions/prejudices/biases are you placing on your new "wine" for this decade? Release it and start today by knowing that He loves you exactly as you are....He made you for a unique purpose so get to it, friend!

Let this be your fresh start for opportunities to serve the Lord without hindrances or restrictions. Get rid of the old wineskins!

Love Him, Obey Him, Serve Him!

Jennifer

Prayer Request

....

....

January 3

> "Now to Him who is able to do far more abundantly beyond all we ask or think, according to the power that works within us, to Him be the glory in the church and in Christ Jesus to all generations forever and ever."
>
> **EPHESIANS 3:20-21**

I keep hearing testimony upon testimony of God's goodness and how He provided for people in the middle of a pandemic. What a FAITHFUL God we serve and how grateful I am for His consistency, mercy, and grace. He never fails and His word is Truth.

Just like a bow is drawn back to propel an arrow forward, I believe that last year was a year of being "drawn back" with the energy to spring forward into this new year. Get ready, get ready, get ready!

This is going to be an overflow year! I pray blessings for each one of you and I believe that every struggle, challenge, and obstacle WILL be used to glorify His name.

Friend, keep pressing on and lean into the Lord. He's got your back!

Jennifer

Prayer Request

January 4

> "For you are all children of the light and of the day; you don't belong to darkness and night."
>
> **1 THESSALONIANS 5:5**

Are you watching what you eat right now after the holidays? Counting calories, analyzing every piece of food that comes into your mouth? And all junk food is banned from your pantry and your plate, I'm sure!

In the same way, we should guard our hearts and minds from receiving "junk" as a part of our daily diet. Guard your eyes from watching or reading anything that would be harmful to your well-being. Junk In equals Junk Out! What you take into your system will be what will define you.

Remember WHO saved your life-JESUS! Now it's time to give your life back to Him by living your best life!

Jennifer

Prayer Request

....

....

January 5

"For we live by believing and not by seeing."

2 CORINTHIANS 5:7

Do you have dreams that you are waiting to see to come to fruition? Do you merely wish for it or do you actively make plans for it? Do you believe that God placed that dream in your heart? Does it glorify Him?

Friend, it's time to move beyond wishing and dreaming. Put some action behind it:

1. PRAY
2. Seek God's Will
3. Embrace the Vision of it
4. JUST GET STARTED!

It's time to move forward in the direction that the Lord wants to place you in your future. Now is the time to get on with it.

Jennifer

Prayer Request

January 6

"She goes to inspect a field and buys it; with her earnings she plants a vineyard. She is energetic and strong, a hard worker. She makes sure her dealings are profitable; her lamp burns into the night."

PROVERBS 31:16-18

Being a hard worker is biblical. Our time on this earth is limited and each day is important. Use your resources well to encourage and edify others. Use your time on this earth to bring others into the Kingdom of God.

Whatever gifts, abilities, and talents that God placed in you, it is your responsibility to develop and use to bless others. What is in your life that can be used to bless others?

Jennifer

Prayer Request

January 7

"But thanks be to God, who always leads us as captives in Christ's triumphal procession and uses us to spread the aroma of HIM everywhere."

2 CORINTHIANS 2:14

Have you ever been around someone who wore too much perfume? Did it trigger a headache, sinus issues, watering eyes? What about emptying a trash can? Did the stench of rotted food cause you to be nauseous?

In the alternative, you ever patiently waited for fresh baked cookies or fresh baked bread in your oven? Did that smell trigger a rumbling tummy in anticipation of eating something delicious?

Friend, our actions leave behind an "aroma" for others to smell. Are you kind and considerate? Gentle and humble? Gracious and forgiving? Tolerant and peaceful? Compassionate and sincere? Loving and merciful?

Let your own personal "aroma" be reflective of the actions of Jesus Christ, which is definitely something that others want to smell!

Jennifer

Prayer Request

January 8

"May you experience the love of Christ, though it is too great to understand fully. Then you will be made complete with all the fullness of life and power that comes from God."

EPHESIANS 3:19

God is love. And He loves everyone. That's right, friend, EVERYONE! Every person, everywhere, at all times.

He doesn't want us to try to fit an illusion of being perfect. He simply wants us to surrender our hearts to Him. TODAY.

Deciding to give your heart to the Creator is the best decision you'll ever make in this side of eternity.

Jennifer

Prayer Request

January 9

"For God has not given us a spirit of fear and timidity, but of power, love, and self-discipline.

2 TIMOTHY 1:7

As believers, we are secure in the knowledge of where we will spend eternity. We have received the gift of eternal life. YAY!

But what do we do while we are still on this earth? How do we deal with our daily decisions, big decisions, or those everyday life dramas?

We have been given many gifts from God. He directs and guides us on the best plan for our lives, empowering and enabling us to fulfill His will for us.

He gives us the spirit of power, love, and self-discipline. FEAR is not of God.

I encourage you to release your faith and put some actions behind your FAITH. Stand strong, believe in the promises of God, seek His will in all that you do, and know that He has got you in the palm of His hand.

Jennifer

Prayer Request

January 10

"I know all the things you do. I have seen your hard work and patient endurance. I know you don't tolerate evil people. You have examined the claims of those who say they are apostles but are not. You have discovered they are liars. You have patiently suffered for Me without quitting."

2 REVELATION 2-3

Wow! This scripture in Revelations was written so many years ago but still holds truth for today's lifestyle.

Friend, as a believer in Christ, you ARE different. You are going to be challenged and ridiculed and even mocked for your beliefs. You will have your own family and friends tell you that believing in an afterlife is pointless. You will be faced with difficult moral dilemmas. You will be told that being positive is ridiculous, especially in adverse situations. You will be told that your faith is silly, meaningless and there is no hope. And if you haven't faced these challenges, just know that you will at some point. You will.

Those negative statements of disbelief are all lies! We do have hope. We do have a future. We do have an afterlife and it's very very real. We have faith and when we combine our ACTIONS with our FAITH, it produces results.

Jennifer

Prayer Request

....

....

January 11

> "But I have this complaint against you. You don't love Me or each other as you did at first! Look how far you have fallen! Turn back to Me and the works you did at first."
>
> **REVELATION 2: 5**

When Paul wrote to the various newly established churches, He was encouraging and edifying them for spiritual growth. The same edification process applies to us today.

When you initially gave your heart to Jesus, loving others was so much easier, wasn't it? Most likely, LOVE simply flowed from your newly redeemed, extremely grateful heart. And then, life happened.

As time passes, it becomes more of a chore to love those who annoy, demean, or disrespect you. Daily living presents challenges to love ALL those around you but know that with God's love and grace, you CAN do it! God is WITH you in every interaction you have in every situation in your life.

Dwell on Him, His promises, His sacrifice, His resurrection power, and He will equip you with the grace to love ALL people.

Jennifer

Prayer Request

January 12

"Come and listen to My counsel. I'll share My heart with you and make you wise."

PROVERBS 1:23

I love God's heart. I know this seems rather simplistic but it's true. I LOVE His heart.

It brings such comfort to me to know that He loves me exactly the way I am right now at this exact moment without any pretense, without any rituals, without anything except bringing my heart to Him. Just my heart and His heart together.

He created me in His image and calls me His child. He forgives me and He has a good plan for me. He enables me, equips me, empowers me, and encourages me in my daily life. He steadies me, sustains me, and showers me with His mercy. He is a good God and He is gracious.

Friend, no matter what you've done and no matter where you are in life, know this fact: GOD loves YOU. Accept His love and let Him dwell in your heart.

Jennifer

Prayer Request

January 13

"My child, listen to what I say, and treasure My commands. Tune your ears to wisdom, and concentrate on understanding."

PROVERBS 2:1-2

I remember many years ago hearing someone say that everyone's favorite radio station dial in their brain is set to "WIIFM", or referred to as What's In It For Me? Literally meaning that every single thought we have is filtered through a WIIFM mentality.

Before you start disagreeing with me, I challenge you to ask yourself.... what are my true motives behind my thoughts and actions? How am I reacting to certain situations.... from a position of compassion, empathy, love, mercy? Or am I reacting from a place of fear, pride, gluttony, and/or selfishness? Quiet yourself and ask yourself these questions to determine the truth. It hurts, doesn't it?

Friend, we are ALL human and we ALL have selfish desires. We ALL listen to the "WIIFM" radio station sometimes. We ALL do!

Just remember that we have an incredible, loving, merciful Father in heaven who wants us to "tune into" Him and His wisdom. Reach out to Him today.

Jennifer

Prayer Request

January 14

"Receive the Holy Spirit. If you forgive anyone's sins, they are forgiven. If you do not forgive them, they are not forgiven."

JOHN 20:22

This scripture passage occurs immediately after Jesus appeared to the disciples after His resurrection, where he greeted them with PEACE first.

Friend, don't you think that any words spoken by Jesus, especially some of the very first words of Jesus after His resurrection, are words that we should allow to resonate within us? Jesus instructed the disciples to be filled with the Holy Spirit, forgive sins, and then He sent them out Into the world.

How do those "instructions" pertain to us as believers today? First, accept Jesus into your heart and know where you will spend eternity. Dwell on His promises that are all throughout the Bible, which will fill you with His peace.

Second, be filled with the Holy Spirit, allowing Him to cleanse your heart, your thoughts, and your actions. If you ask for the Holy Spirit to guide you, direct you, counsel you, convict you, and comfort you, trust me. He will do it.

Third, show up every day as a witness for Christ and His great love for people. Does this mean you must be perfectly behaved, always dressed professionally, reading the Bible 24 hours a day, hanging out only at your church? No! Be YOURSELF, loving God, loving and forgiving others, and trusting Him to guide you to those He places in your path.

Jennifer

Prayer Request

....

....

January 15

"And Jesus replied, 'I assure you, today you will be with Me in paradise.'"

LUKE 23:43

Jesus was crucified in between two criminals. One criminal mocked Jesus while the other criminal repented and believed in Jesus as the Son of God. Even while He was literally hanging from a cross with nails in his hands and feet, Jesus was still full of compassion, offering redemption and comfort to OTHERS. His focus was never on His own comfort, social status, wealth accumulation, or professional associations. It was ALWAYS about love.

Let me challenge you today: WHAT do you need to do to MOVE OUT OF YOUR OWN COMFORT zone to help someone else? Whom can you encourage by writing an uplifting note or email? Can you bring a meal to someone or have a meal delivered for someone who is unable to shop for themselves? Whom can you bless financially? Whom can you pray for on a regular and consistent basis? Can you drive someone to their doctor's office for appointments? Who needs groceries? It's time to GET MOVING!

Jennifer

Prayer Request

January 16

"And do not bring sorrow to God's Holy Sprit by the way you live. Remember, He has identified you as His own, guaranteeing that you will be saved on the day of redemption."

EPHESIANS 4:30

I do not know about you, but I am radically opposed to someone telling me what NOT to do! I'm not rebellious but I do like to make my own decisions and follow my "gut instincts" in many situations. Having said that, I also want to have a clean heart before the Lord. So, friends, the struggle is REAL for me at times!

Instead of focusing on the "should not" and "shall not" aspects of making major decisions, I choose to focus on what is truly going to please God. He is whom I want to please and He is my very best friend.

In my own strength and knowledge, do I always make the best life decisions? Nope.

Do I TRY to make wise decisions, leaning on the wisdom from the Lord, listening to the sage advice of experienced counsel, using my own experiences and education combined with the leading of the Holy Spirit? That is my goal. And every day I learn something new about God and myself. Remember, this is a journey!

Jennifer

Prayer Request

....

....

January 17

"Now the Lord has brought it about; He has done just as He said He would."

JEREMIAH 40:3

In these unprecedented times, it is normal to become discouraged or even despair at the world's current pandemic. Our daily routines have been radically altered through local stay-at-home decrees, our careers may seem unsteady in the wake of financial uncertainty, our children's academic success now depends on their ability to learn in online environments, our friendships include creative social distancing activities, our vacation plans have come to a screeching halt, and the list continues....

Despite the uncertainty and despite the chaos, there IS a divine Order to this entire situation! God still sits on the throne, God still changes lives, God still dearly loves each one of us, and God will do what He says He will do.

Read your Bible, let His words resonate with you, pray to Him, and rest in the knowledge that HE HAS YOU IN THE PALM OF HIS HANDS.

Jennifer

Prayer Request

January 18

"Imitate God, therefore, in everything you do, because you are His dear children'

EPHESIANS 5:1

Whom are you "imitating" today?

When my daughter was younger, there was another young lady who always seemed to imitate her various hairstyles. When my daughter would become frustrated about it, I reminded her that the most sincere form of flattery is imitation.

The success of Advertising is built upon each one of us desiring certain products or services. Think about it: What is the current desire of your heart? Whom are you imitating in thoughts, words, or deeds? What products must you possess in order to appear successful, younger, or more desirable to others?

Friend, I am human and I have selfish desires. I like to travel, drink expensive coffees, watch Netflix, wear designer clothes, and go out to dinner, just like you! I love to wear expensive shoes and pretty jewelry, just like you! I love to have kayaking adventures, read self empowerment books, talk on the most recent version of an iPhone, listen to the latest music through fancy air buds, just like you! But hear me, please, hear me: ALL OF IT is temporary and none of it brings true JOY.

This world will not last and ETERNITY is forever. Get your heart right with Jesus.

Jennifer

Prayer Request

....

....

January 19

> "Why am I so honored, that the Mother of my Lord should visit me? When I heard your greeting, the baby in my womb jumped for joy. You are blessed because you believed that the Lord would do what He said."
>
> **LUKE 1:43-45**

What an honor that Mary visited her cousin, Elizabeth (who was pregnant with John the Baptist) while she was pregnant with Jesus! John the Baptist literally leapt in the womb in the presence of the Lord.

How excited are you about the presence of Jesus in your life today? Does He bring you joy? Does He bring you peace? Do you love spending time with Him, allowing Him to re-energize you and direct you on the best path for your life?

Call out to Him, acknowledge your need for Him, surrender your heart to Him, and let Him make His presence known in your life.

Jennifer

Prayer Request

January 20

"Then Jesus called to the crowd to come and hear.
"All of you listen', he said, 'and try to understand.
It's not what goes into your body that defiles you;
you are defiled by what comes from your heart."

MARK 7: 14-16

Have you heard the phrase, "Junk In equals Junk Out" in reference to what you eat? I submit to you that the same phrase applies to our minds and hearts.

If you dwell on resentment, bitterness, jealousy, revenge, gossip, spreading rumors, telling lies, harboring a grudge, sexual immorality, or plotting evil schemes, you will begin to place "splinters" of unhappiness in your heart. Friend, you were created for more than living a life with "splinters" in your heart! The Lord wants you to have unspeakable joy in Him.

Ask God to give you the wisdom and the strength to heal from every situation in your life that causes you to have those "splinters" in your heart. Take some practical steps towards coming up higher in your life: Stop gossiping and spreading rumors. If you're jealous of someone, pray for God to show you how to bless them. If you're involved in sexually immoral conduct, stop It and pray for strength to avoid temptation. If you're telling lies, stop it immediately and ask God to place restraint on your mouth.

Allow God to do what only He can do and then watch Him do it.

Jennifer

Prayer Request

January 21

> "After everyone was full, Jesus told His disciples,' Now gather the leftovers so that nothing is wasted.' So they picked up the pieces and filled twelve baskets with scraps left by the people who had eaten from the five barley loaves."
>
> **JOHN 6: 12-13**

Does God NEED our finances? No, of course not. He's the Creator of the Universe.

Does God WANT us to be obedient to Him and tithe part of our income? Yes.

Is it true that as we reveal to Him that we can be trusted with little, then we will be trusted with more and more? Yes.

Does God want us to TRUST Him that when we show our obedience to Him through our tithes and offerings, He will provide for us? Yes.

Does God want us to give with a GRATEFUL heart? Yes.

Does God want us to make a huge production or showmanship of our generosity? Nope, just do it and know that GOD SEES YOUR GIVING.

Let God show up and show off in your life! He will provide you with MORE than enough!

Jennifer

Prayer Request

January 22

"The eyes of the Lord search the whole earth in order to strengthen those whose hearts are fully committed to Him."

2 CHRONICLES 16:9

A few years ago, I read this verse and it truly resonated with me. It wasn't a verse that I had memorized nor was it a verse that was commonly quoted by others. It was a obscure verse that I recalled reading at some point in my life so I began searching for it, found it, and prayed about it. That same night I attended a presentation at my mother's church and that was the exact same scripture that the speaker highlighted. Coincidence? Nope. It spoke volumes to me that God confirmed what I was dwelling on was from Him and that He was and still is seeking those who are "fully committed" to Him.

Is someone who is "fully committed" to Christ someone who is perfect? No way! We all have areas of weakness, imperfections, character flaws, and things that we need to correct in our behavior/thoughts/attitudes. ALL of us have areas that need refinement from the Holy Spirit.

This week that same obscure passage came to mind again, and I believe that God is making Himself known to the unbelievers and the believers. For the unbelievers, it is time to begin a relationship with Him. And for those who already know Him, it's time to lean into Him, trust Him, be "fully committed" to Him, and let HIM strengthen us.

Jennifer

Prayer Request

January 23

> "A righteous man may have many troubles,
> but the Lord delivers him from them all."
>
> **PSALM 34:19**

Are you in trouble right now? Is the state of our nation's health crisis causing you emotional or financial strain? Are you feeling anxious, alone, or depressed? You have an Advocate and His name is Jesus. Reach out to Him.

I also encourage you to proactively reach out to your community of believers. The church isn't just the building....it's the COMMUNITY of common believers who are here to assist, encourage, and edify one another. If you're looking for a church, start with online communities. There are online churches, bible studies, and support groups in abundance. Reach out to others today to encourage and edify on another as we journey through life together.

Jennifer

Prayer Request

January 24

"Be still and know that I am God."

PSALM 46:10

Are you naturally a worrier? Do you sweat the small stuff? Are you a planner, a "busy bee", an individual who loves to organize? Do you detest laziness? Is a good day for you a day in which you hit the ground running with a list of to-do items?

The more I learn to truly trust in Jesus, the more I find myself "resting in the Lord" even in the midst of a hustle-bustle day. And yes, I still abhor laziness but I think there is a balance between working and resting. I encourage you to find your balance today.

Seek first the kingdom of God and ask Him to arrange your priorities and your schedule. If you submit first to His will for your life, you will be amazed at how truly productive you will become while you "rest" in Him.

Jennifer

Prayer Request

January 25

"Love never gives up, never loses faith, is always hopeful, and endured through every circumstance."

1 CORINTHIANS 13:7

Love never fails.

Love never fails.

Love never fails.

Mocked by a crowd, Beaten by whips, Nailed to a cross, Buried in a borrowed tomb, Three days later..... LOVE NEVER FAILS!

If you haven't surrendered your heart to Jesus yet, I encourage you to do it today. Don't wait to give your heart to the Creator. He is waiting to receive you just as you are, without judgment and without condemnation.

LOVE NEVER FAILS!

Jennifer

Prayer Request

January 26

"I can do all things through Christ who strengthens me."

PHILIPPIANS 4:13

We are in turbulent times as a global society. The COVID pandemic has affected everything from daily activities to impacting the global economy.

In these turbulent times, know WHO is your true source of strength. Know WHO is your provider.

You may be thinking to yourself that you provide for yourself because you get up everyday and go to work. While there is truth to that belief that you are working hard for your income, it is GOD who provides the health, the energy, the resources, the opportunities, the "right" connections that you need to earn your income.

Look to HIM first and let Him guide you in every area of your life. Be grateful for the opportunities and the resources He provides for you. And for goodness sake, keep working at whatever He provides for you!

Jennifer

Prayer Request

....

....

January 27

> "We are hard pressed on every side but not crushed; perplexed but not in despair; persecuted but not abandoned; struck down but not destroyed. We always carry around in our body the death of Jesus so that the life of Jesus may also be revealed in our body."
>
> **2 CORINTHIANS 4:8-10**

Are you feeling overwhelmed, anxious, or even angry at the world's current situation? I encourage you to take heart and read that above scripture repeatedly.

Difficult times happen to everyone. Yes, everyone. I believe that the difference in moving to the next level in your life is your reaction to whatever that unique challenge is as it presents itself to you.

There are many situations in life that I think are inherently unfair, truly unjust, or just plain terrible, but this I know to be true: Our God remains in control!

He who began a good work in you will complete it. He loves you, my friend. He Is in control of your life.

He is omniscient. He has not necessarily caused, but has allowed, this difficult situation in your life. Seek His guidance, His wisdom, His grace, His strength, His favor, and you will find His *peace*.

Jennifer

Prayer Request

January 28

"But those who HOPE in the Lord will renew their strength. They will soar on wings like eagles; they will run and not grow weary; they will walk and not grow faint."

ISAIAH 40:31

As I write this, we are in the midst of a pandemic. People are watching new series on Netflix, experimenting with new recipes in the kitchen, and using new apps such as Zoom to communicate with family and friends. Just as we are all adapting to this "new normal" of how we conduct business, purchase groceries, watch online church, participate in online bible studies, communicate with friends, etc, we are realizing that we can still function on a daily basis. We are surviving.

But surviving is NOT the same as thriving. Friend, where is your HOPE? Are you merely going through the motions, wishing that the pandemic (or whatever crisis you're currently in) would end so you can return to your busy and hectic lifestyle?

Don't go through this current pandemic or any other situation with a survival mentality-go through it with a THRIVE mentality! Look up to the Lord to lead and direct you. Place your hope and your trust in the Lord. He will never fail you!

Jennifer

Prayer Request

January 29

"I pray that the eyes of your heart may be enlightened in order that you may know the hope to which He has called you, the riches of His glorious inheritance in His holy people, and His incomparably great power for us who believe."

EPHESIANS 1:18

HOPE. We have hope as believers in Christ! The same power that resurrected Jesus from the grave is available to us as Christians. The same resurrection power!

We serve such a merciful and mighty Lord! He rose from the dead-nothing is too hard for Him. Absolutely nothing intimidates Him or confuses Him. He is THE rock upon which we can build our lives. A firm foundation exists when He is in "first place" in our lives, with everything coming under His authority and His direction.

What situation in your life needs to have some HOPE injected into it? Pray and keep praying!

Jennifer

Prayer Request

January 30

"So he said to me, 'This is the word of the Lord to Zerubbabel: Not by might nor by power but by My Spirit' says the Lord Almighty."

ZECHARIAH 4:6

Might.

Power.

Spirit.

Three very distinct words. Which one seems to carry the most impact to you? Which one appears to show weakness? Which one is the word that you use when you describe the Lord?

The Holy Spirit is powerful and dwells in us as believers. The Holy Spirit is our Counselor, our Guide, our Comforter, our Conscience (convicts us), our Teacher, and many other wonderful descriptive attributes.

If you need a special dose of God's love today, I encourage you to reach out to the Lord in prayer and believe that He will answer you!

Jennifer

Prayer Request

January 31

"If we are thrown into the blazing furnace, the God we serve is able to deliver us from it."

DANIEL 3:17

Shadrach, Meshach, and Abednego were ordered to be thrown into a blazing furnace by King Nebuchadnezzar. These three young Jewish men refused to worship the King's golden idols or any other false gods. In a rage, the King ordered the furnace to be heated seven times hotter than normal and for each man to be tightly bound as they were thrown into the fire.

These courageous young men remained true to God, to the point of refusing to defend themselves and stating that God would deliver them from being killed in the furnace. And deliver them He did! For more details, I encourage you to read Daniel 3:4-30.

After all three young men emerged from the fire unharmed without even the smell of smoke on their clothing, King Nebuchadnezzar began praising the Lord, to include issuing a decree that the Lord's name would be protected.

This story is not a fairy tale but rather a historical account of God's awesome power! Let this remind you today that we serve a truly awesome God!

Jennifer

Prayer Request

FEBRUARY

"Then you will call upon Me and come and pray to Me, and I will listen to you. You will seek Me and find Me when you seek Me with all of your heart. I will be found by you!"

Jeremiah 29:12-14

February 1

> "Then you will call upon Me and come and pray to Me, and I will listen to you. You will seek Me and find Me when you seek Me with all of your heart. I will be found by you!"
>
> **JEREMIAH 29: 12-14**

When you were a child, were you instructed to stay close to your parent if you went out in public? Did you tightly hold your parent's hand or did you run wild in stores?

As a mama, I always instructed my children to hold my hand whenever we crossed the street or were in a public place. Why did I tell them to do this? To keep them safe. To shield them from possible incoming danger. To guide them on the best path.

It is the same way with our Heavenly Father. Hold tightly to His hand as He guides you, protects you, and shields you.

Jennifer

Prayer Request

....

....

February 2

"Is anything too hard for the Lord?"

GENESIS 18:14

Abraham is often named the "Father of many nations." This particular scripture listed above is found in Genesis in reference to when Sarah (Abraham's wife) laughed after hearing that she, an elderly woman, was going to finally become pregnant. She literally laughed at a promise from God. This wasn't a laugh a delight but rather a laugh of scorn and bitterness. Have you ever done this In response to something that the Lord has promised you?

Know this fact: God wins! Every. Single. Time.

Before you shake your head in that Sarah would doubt what God promised her, I encourage you to reflect on your own actions. What dreams or promises has God impressed upon you that you've given up on and become bitter instead? Sometimes it is actually easier to embrace the negative words spoken to us but now is the time to change thought patterns, starting with your own heart and the word of God. Read your Bible and let the Holy Spirit fill you with wisdom.

Jennifer

Prayer Request

February 3

> "Be anxious for nothing, but in everything by prayer and supplication with thanksgiving, let your requests be made known to God. And the peace of God, which passes all comprehension will guard your hearts and your minds in Christ Jesus."
>
> **PHILIPPIANS 4:6-7**

Praise the Lord! That's right, you heard me, PRAISE the Lord!

When you praise Him for WHO He is (Savior, faithful, generous, loving, kind, compassionate, Provider, wise counselor, omniscient, best friend, powerful, Redeemer, Healer, Waymaker, the Alpha and the Omega). Before you bring your petitions to Him, you've created an atmosphere for true worship. Praise Him! Praise Him! Praise Him!

Talk to Jesus about what's on your heart. He is the Lord but He is also your friend. When praise proceeds your petitions, victory will result in your life!

Jennifer

Prayer Request

....

....

February 4

"Now this is the confidence that we have in Him, that if we ask anything according to His will, He hears us. And if we know that He hears us, whatever we ask, we know that we have the petitions that we have asked of Him."

1 JOHN 5:14-15

Are there prayers that you seem to place on the "repeat" cycle, constantly going to the Lord and asking the exact same request? Do you feel like your prayers are going unheard and unanswered? Does this delay create doubt in your mind about whether or not the Lord loves you?

When it seems as if He isn't answering you, you're in good company! There are numerous times where I have been impatient for Him to answer my prayers but I have learned that He hears me and He is working on the solution. Many of us become impatient for our prayers to be answered but it is true that He hears us and will respond in His timing.

KNOW this fact: He hears you. He sees you. He loves you. And keep praying. He is always there, and He is faithful.

Jennifer

Prayer Request

February 5

"There is a time for everything, and a season for every activity under the heavens."

ECCLESIASTES 3:1

Are you missing something or someone today? Do you have wonderful memories made with family or friends? Do you review old photographs and laugh at the clothing choices? Reflect on the past but please don't live there! Life is going on right now and there is no "pause" button.

I've heard it said repeatedly that some people enter your life for a reason and some people are there just for a season. I believe that is true!

A significant relationship of mine ended recently last year leaving many unanswered questions. While the end of that relationship brought confusion, it also brought unbelievable clarity in so many other areas of my life, to include deeper trust in the Lord, increased commitment to family relationships, more time on my calendar to strengthen bonds of friendship with others, an renewed exuberance in exercise, a dedication to daily prayer, and a peace that has truly passed all understanding.

Has it been challenging? Yes.

But has it been worth it now?

Yes, and what a tremendous BLESSING it has been to learn that the Lord is faithful all the time.

Jennifer

Prayer Request

February 6

> "I will give them an undivided heart and put a new spirit in them; I will remove from them their heart of stone and give them a heart of flesh."
>
> **EZEKIEL 11:19**

It's time for a heart transplant! Do you harbor resentment, bitterness, selfish ambition, doubt, or have regrets over certain situations? If so, you're in good company!

Friend, let's exchange those negative emotions for the life-giving spirit that will heal us and make us truly whole. And when we are healed, the same situations that "tested" us will become our "testimonies" to God's goodness. He IS faithful and He is a good, good Father! Yay for the Lord, our Jehovah Rapha (our healer)!

Jennifer

Prayer Request

February 7

"I always thank my God as I remember you in my prayers because I hear about your love for all His holy people and your faith in Jesus Christ."

PHILEMON 4

What an incredible gift Philemon received when Paul wrote these words to him! To receive such a word of encouragement from a committed and humble servant of the Lord must have been inspirational indeed!

Friend, I encourage you to examine your own life. Are you living for Christ or for yourself? Are you dedicating your time to advancing His kingdom or your own personal agenda? Does your future planning involve His Will and purpose for your life? Please don't misunderstand my questions as directed exclusively to you... I am reflecting on them as well.

I am praying for each of us right now as I write this that God will provide fresh vision and anointing on each one of us as we live out our purpose for His glory.

Jennifer

Prayer Request

February 8

"Take delight in the Lord and He will give you the desires of your heart."

PSALM 37:4

This scripture verse has a completely different meaning for me as I mature as a believer in Jesus Christ.

At first glance, this scripture could be interpreted as "love the Lord and He will give you whatever you want", similar to a Santa Claus or a Genie in a Bottle scenario.

Here's another way to read that scripture: LOVE the Lord (fully commit to Him, live to please Him, acknowledge Him as Lord in every area of your life) and your heart's desires will become the same as the Lord's desires for your life. Delight in pleasing Him!

As you live for Him, your heart will begin to beat in rhythm with the Lord's desires for your life. He is a good, good Father.

Jennifer

Prayer Request

February 9

"The light shines in the darkness and the darkness can never extinguish it."

JOHN 1:5

What dark corners of your life need some light shown? Whether it's as simple as a flashlight shining onto a dark path in the woods or as majestic as the sun rising every morning, the dark must give way to the light! The LIGHT wins every time!

I encourage you today to speak God's truth over every single area of your life. And as you continue to confess God's TRUTH into your own circumstances, watch your life begin to change.

Jennifer

Prayer Request

February 10

"For the Lord gives wisdom, and from His mouth come knowledge and understanding."

PROVERBS 2:6

Education is important and vital to success in today's world. Wisdom, however, is often underrated.

Jesus frequently surrounded himself with people whom the world would view as being of lowly social status : fishermen and craftsmen, even a tax collector! Why did He do this? He came to save ALL, not just the wealthy or "successful" people.

His disciples were predominantly uneducated, humble people whom the Lord imparted incredible wisdom and courage as they spread the Gospel after his resurrection.

Jesus, the King of Kings and Lord of Lords, was born to a modest and simple young woman and placed in a manger. Complete humility in his birth yet 2,000 years later He is still making a difference. Wise people still seek Him!

Jennifer

Prayer Request

February 11

"I pray that God, the source of hope, will fill you completely with joy and peace because you trust in Him. Then you will overflow with confident hope through the power of the Holy Spirit."

ROMANS 15:13

There is a old saying that I used to hear repeatedly, "Birds of a feather flock together." Basically meaning that likeminded people will congregate together. So ask yourself this important question: who is in my flock? With whom do I socialize, exercise, work, travel, etc?

As believers, we can place our trust in God, who will fill our lives with His goodness as we dwell in His presence. And how do you "dwell" in His presence? By spending time with Him!

Are you spending time with the Lord on a daily basis? I have discovered in my own life that the more time I spend in His presence, the more my entire life becomes a reflection of His characteristics. My daily goal is to seek Him and please Him.

Jennifer

Prayer Request

February 12

"Lord, there is no one like You! For You are great, and Your name is full of power."

JEREMIAH 10:6

Are there certain last names in your hometown that have distinction? For instance, in my hometown there are several multi-generational names that carry significant weight due to their contributions to the construction or development of our area. Those specific last names have recognition within our community.

In the same context, the Lord's name has instant recognition. As children of God, we therefore have His name: CHRISTians. And we have His favor, His protection, and His distinct calling upon our lives. You have been given unique gifts and abilities. It is your responsibility to develop those talents. I encourage you to use your time on this earth wisely to help others and demonstrate His love. We have opportunities each day to serve others.

CHRISTIANS.

Wear the name well, sisters and brothers!

Jennifer

Prayer Request

February 13

"Trust in the Lord with all of your heart, do not depend on your own understanding. Seek His will in all that you do, and He will show you which path to take."

PROVERBS 3:5-6

Isn't it refreshing that our Lord is completely trustworthy, completely dependable, and completely reliable? I encourage you to trust Him, seek Him, and then allow Him to guide you each day in making the best decisions for every situation.

From a practical standpoint, you may be asking, how do you begin trusting Him to guide you? Spend time in His presence, allowing Him to fill you with His peace and His love. When you spend time with Him each day, your heart grows, and your mind becomes renewed with Christ's teachings. He is worthy to be praised and His word is true to guide us.

Jennifer

Prayer Request

February 14

"You have come to Jesus, the One who mediates the new covenant between God and people, and to the sprinkled blood, which speaks of forgiveness instead of crying out for vengeance like the blood of Abel."

HEBREWS 12:24

What is your definition of TRUE LOVE? Whatever it is, know this: There is no one who will love you more than the Lord. He is your Creator. He designed you for a purpose and gave His only Son for you.

He gave up His only Son. Let that sink into your Spirit. He loves you so much! Let Him be your true Valentine. When you give Him your heart, He will protect it and guard it. His covenant with you is everlasting. You are His precious child and He loves you.

Jennifer

Prayer Request

February 15

"Be silent before the Lord, all humanity, for He is springing into action from His holy dwelling."

ZECHARIAH 2:13

None of the chaos and disharmony in the world has taken God by surprise. None of it! He is sovereign, He is the Creator, and He is omniscient.

Now is the time to pray, to ask for guidance and wisdom in how to navigate through the world we live in today. Seek His will for your life, reach out to those who are hurting, work hard at your vocational calling, spend time with your loved ones, and cherish every moment. Christian leadership BEGINS in your own heart and with your own family.

Whenever you feel despair at the disorder, know that there is a divine order above the chaos. And pray that peace will prevail! He is the God of justice. At just the right time, the Lord will make it happen.

Jennifer

Prayer Request

February 16

"Therefore, whenever we have the opportunity,
we should do good to everyone-especially
those in the family of faith."

GALATIANS 6:10

Do you do good to other people on a consistent basis? If you see a need, do you try to fill it? For instance, if you know someone who is looking for a new job and you hear about an opportunity that might be a good fit for them, do you take the time to make that connection for them? If you know someone is struggling in their finances, do you offer to assist them by bringing groceries, helping pay a utility bill, or assist them in creating a household budget for them to get out of debt?

When you see opportunities to help others, DO IT! Friend, this is the time and this is the season to help others more than ever. Start with little things if you feel intimidated but please start somewhere!

When you go to dinner, tip more than necessary. Waiters and waitresses may be struggling to make ends meet in their home budgets. When you think about purchasing fresh produce, buy some extra for your neighbors and hand-deliver it to them. When you go to the dollar store, pick up some extra toothpaste, toothbrushes, shampoo, soap, and make bags of these items for the homeless.

We have been so blessed and we are blessed to BE a blessing to others!

Jennifer

Prayer Request

February 17

> "To all who mourn in Israel, He will give a crown of beauty for ashes, a joyous blessing instead of mourning, festive praise instead of despair. In their righteousness, they will be like great oaks that the Lord has planted for His own glory."
>
> **ISAIAH 61:3**

Whatever you're dealing with, whatever "IT" is, whatever concerns you have right now, I encourage you to GIVE IT to the Lord. He's got it!

When you feel discouraged or alone, know that He is right there beside you. He's your biggest fan and He loves you.

Have you been discouraged because of an unfair situation? Has someone lied about you, talked behind your back, broken your heart, or destroyed your enthusiasm for life? Pick your head up and smile because the Lord will vindicate you.

Jennifer

Prayer Request

....

....

February 18

> "The smallest family will become a thousand people,
> and the tiniest group will become a mighty nation.
> At the right time, I, the Lord, will make it happen."
>
> **ISAIAH 60:22**

Waiting on the Lord is not easy. If you're anything like me, I have a lot of natural energy! I still get excited about taking a vacation, going on a new adventure, starting a project, or meeting a new friend.

Whenever I truly believe that God is wanting me to wait on making a decision or proceeding in a certain area of my life, I have learned it is best to do just that: Wait on the Lord for His guidance.

This does not come naturally to me because of my energy level and the fact that I am very goal-oriented; however, when I heed that instruction, I know that I'm walking in His will for my life. His will is the best way to live!

Pray about whatever decisions/obstacles you're facing and listen to the gentle leading of the Lord. Read your Bible and absorb some heavenly wisdom. He will multiply your dreams and increase your opportunities if you simply trust Him to do it His way. Pursue your dreams, work diligently, be faithful and trustworthy, and trust Him to do what you cannot do in your own efforts. HE IS ABLE!

Jennifer

Prayer Request

February 19

"What good is it, dear brothers and sisters, if you say you have faith but don't show it by your actions? Can that kind of faith save anyone?"

JAMES 2:14

Whom is God calling you to help today? Don't wait, don't overthink it, just do it! If He places someone on your heart, reach out to them. Let Him guide you to the people who need your assistance.

Deliver food, pay a utility bill, take them out to dinner, bring them clothing, help them with housework, whatever God is showing you to do.... JUST DO IT! When we are obedient to the prompting of the Holy Spirit, it will frequently require us to leave our comfort zone. If you have a genuine desire to help others, you need to move your feet to begin serving others and responding to the call of the Lord.

Our faith is an active faith so please put some actions behind your words!

Jennifer

Prayer Request

February 20

> "Now all glory to God, who is ABLE, through His mighty power at work within us, to accomplish infinitely more than we might ask or think."
>
> **EPHESIANS 3:20**

Our God is ABLE to do it! He is still in the miracle working business and He wants you to acknowledge Him when those dreams come to fruition. Reflect on your past when He has made a way for you. He is still the same God and He will do it again!

Give your dreams to the Lord. Fully surrender your heart's desires and your own timeline to Him. His timing and His way!

Pray hard, work hard, and TRUST in the One who loves you so!

Jennifer

Prayer Request

February 21

"In view of all this, make every effort to respond to God's promises. Supplement your faith with a generous provision of moral excellence and moral excellence with knowledge and knowledge with self-control and self-control with patient endurance and patient endurance with godliness and godliness with brotherly affection and brotherly affection with love for everyone."

2 PETER 1: 5-7

That scripture verse can seem daunting at first glance! Wow! It clearly outlines behavior attributes that I do not possess on a regular and consistent basis.

BUT THIS IS A FACT: I've made up my mind to set the bar high for myself in every area of my life, to include my commitment to the Lord. It's a daily commitment to renew my mind and my heart to Him and submit to His will for my life. This is the way I choose to live my life for the rest of my life. It's not a pursuit of perfection, which would be an exercise in futility, but rather a pursuit of becoming excellent. Every day mistakes are made and every day I seek to improve my life.

This scripture is a goal of behavior for me as a believer in Christ.

Jennifer

Prayer Request

February 22

"Should people cheat God? Yet you have cheated Me! But you ask, 'What do you mean? When did we ever cheat you?' You have cheated me of the tithes and offerings due to me."

MALACHI 3:8

This verse is not a comforting one to me. It is a verse of instruction of obedience and discipline. I am a natural spender and not a natural saver. I don't consider myself a selfish person but when it comes to tithing the full 10 percent of my income on a regular and consistent basis, it takes a commitment that I often shrink away from in fear. Fear of not having enough, fear of missing out on fun experiences because I would give away all of my income, or basically fear that God wouldn't take care of me.

I can come up with some terrific excuses to not give the full tithe of my income. How about you? Just start doing it. Any amount to get started, trusting God to protect your finances. And keep watching the tithing amount increase and God's protection continue to watch over your family's finances. He says that we can actually test Him in this matter so begin tithing and trust Him to provide for you! (Malachi 3:10)

Jennifer

Prayer Request

February 23

> "He sent me to comfort the broken-hearted and to proclaim that captives will be released and prisoners will be freed. He has sent me to tell those who mourn that the time of the Lord's favor has come, and with it, the day of God's anger against their enemies."
>
> **ISAIAH 61:1-2**

Have you waited and waited for something to happen in your life? Perhaps it's a new relationship, a new career , a business venture, an investment opportunity, a retirement plan, health condition healed, a mortgage-free home, increased salary, an educational opportunity for you or a loved one, an international trip, etc..

Whatever "IT" is, think about how excited you'll be when it actually occurs!

As believers, we should be just that excited about our salvation and our eternal destination.

THIS WORLD IS NOT OUR FINAL DESTINATION... we are headed somewhere much better when our time on this earth ends. Just knowing that fact should bring a huge smile to your face!

If you're dealing with any kind of "heaviness" today, be comforted. This will pass, my friend. Trust the Lord and His plan for your life. Everything has a season and this time of mourning will pass. The Lord is taking care of you.

Jennifer

Prayer Request

....

....

February 24

"Instead of shame and dishonor, you will enjoy a double share of honor. You will possess a double portion of prosperity in your land and everlasting joy will be yours."

ISAIAH 61:7

Have you ever been through a tough time in your life? If so, did the tough time seem endless? I have been through some tough times in my life and some common phrases that I would hear is "tough times don't last but tough people do" and "hang in there" and "this too shall pass" and many more of similar nature.

While those common phrases did encourage me for brief periods of time, it was scripture verses that actually SUSTAINED me. Scripture verses that I wrote down on slips of paper, posted them everywhere I could rehearse them, and knew them by heart.

The verse above was one of those verses. I truly believed (and still do) that God is a Redeemer. Friend, whatever you're facing today, I encourage you to pray, seek God's will for your life, fall on your knees in true and heartfelt worship of Him, let Him RESTORE and REDEEM you! We serve an AWESOME God.

Jennifer

Prayer Request

February 25

> "Everyone who acknowledges me publicly here on earth, I will also acknowledge before My Father in heaven. But everyone who denies Me here on earth, I will also deny before My Father in heaven."
>
> **MATTHEW 10:32-33**

Our time on this earth is not to be wasted. What gifts, talents, and resources have you been given by the Lord? Use them well!

When you use what you have been given (talent, abilities, skills, resources), you will be blessed with more each day. Apply wisdom and discernment as to how to best use what God has given you to promote His kingdom.

Our hope is eternal because of our faith in Jesus and we have an obligation to share our faith and hope with others. Heaven is not reserved solely for us and it's not an exclusive "club." Jesus died for ALL of us. Go ahead and invite others to love the Lord!

Jennifer

Prayer Request

February 26

> "In view of all of this, make every effort to respond to God's promises. Supplement your faith with a generous provision of moral excellence, and moral excellence with knowledge, and knowledge with self-control, and self-control with patient endurance, and patient endurance with godliness and godliness with brotherly affection, and brotherly affection with love for everyone."
>
> **2 PETER 1:5-7**

God has given us everything we need to live life His way. When we give our hearts to Him and begin to trust Him to take care of us, we can learn to walk by FAITH. He watches over us, protects us, and guides us. He is a good, good, good Father.

Nothing is impossible for the Lord. Nothing! And He is concerned about our everyday needs as well as our more serious needs. Daily communication with Him through prayer will connect you to the best power source: His AWESOME Power!

When we are truly connected to Him, a new strength will arise in us and love for others will flow forth. I encourage you to get "charged up" in the presence of the Lord. He is and always will be the true source of everlasting joy, peace, grace, mercy, wisdom, and power.

Jennifer

Prayer Request

February 27

> "Pay careful attention to your own work, for then you will get the satisfaction of a job well done and you won't need to compare yourself to anyone else. For we are each responsible for our own conduct."
>
> **GALATIANS 6:4**

When you are at work, do you try your best? Or do you do only the bare minimum, loafing around the rest of the work day? Do you play games on your work computer instead of actually doing your work?

Friend, YOU are responsible for your own conduct. Don't "pass the buck" or play the "blame game" for your own laziness. Give your work your very best effort. Having gainful employment is a gift from God.

This doesn't mean that you have to be a "perfect" employee but rather one who is always trying their best to do a good job, learning from mistakes, and possessing integrity in all dealings with others.

Jennifer

Prayer Request

February 28

> "Blessings on the King who comes in the name of the Lord! Peace in heaven, and glory in highest heaven!"
>
> **LUKE 19:38**

People all have opinions. Sometimes their opinions change as frequently as the direction the wind blows on a particular day. Depending on their mood or overall attitude towards life, their opinion can shift without any basis.

When Jesus rode the colt into the Jerusalem on what we now refer to as Palm Sunday, the crowds were praising and exalting His name as the King. A few days later, the crowd was filled with hate, taunting insults and wanting to crucify Him.

After Jesus was crucified and buried in a borrowed tomb, He rose from the dead. The grave couldn't hold Him!

He remains alive today and as believers, we have that resurrection power, grace, love, and mercy available to us. Reach out to Him through prayer and ask Him to dwell in your heart.

Let your heart be renewed with faith today.

Jennifer

Prayer Request

MARCH

"We are confident of all this because of our great trust in God through Christ. It is not that we think that we are qualified to do anything on our own. Our qualification comes from God."

2 Corinthians 3:4

March 1

"We are confident of all this because of our great trust in God through Christ. It is not that we think that we are qualified to do anything on our own. Our qualification comes from God."

2 CORINTHIANS 3:4

If you think you're in the wrong position at your place of employment or at your place of worship, consider this verse. Your qualification comes from the Lord!

Acknowledge Him in EVERY single area of your life and follow His leading as to what steps are next. You may need to receive more education, more networking options, different location, but FIRST, do this simple act: pause, PRAY, and ask God for clear direction and guidance. He will give it to you!

Jennifer

Prayer Request

....

....

March 2

"I will put my instructions deep within them, and I will write them on their hearts. I will be their God and they will be My people."

JEREMIAH 31:33

When you purchase an item that has to be assembled at home, do you actually read the instructions? Do you ask others for assistance? Do you become frustrated or is it easy for you to assemble items without instructions? I frequently become frustrated when I have to assemble an item that I purchased; however, if I take the time to read the instructions, it is a much smoother process. In the same way, when we slow down and read the bible to absorb God's plan for our lives, we have clarity and purpose.

When you are a follower of the Lord, your heart belongs to Him. Allow His instructions to be written on your heart.

He will lead you and He will guide you on the BEST path for your life.

TRUST Him!

Jennifer

Prayer Request

March 3

> "Now this is the confidence that we have in Him, that if we ask anything according to His will, He hears us. And if we know that He hears us, whatever we ask, we know that we have the petitions that we have asked of Him."
>
> **1 JOHN 5:14-15**

God is not a genie in a bottle who grants our every wish. He is not Santa and He is not the tooth fairy. While these are sweet notions, the fact remains that God is sovereign and His ways are not our ways.

He is GOD and He is GOOD! Trust Him with every single area of your life. While we don't understand His methods or His ways, He has a master plan for our lives. Trusting Him becomes a way of life the more we see examples of His continued faithfulness exemplified in our lives.

Jennifer

Prayer Request

. . . .

. . . .

March 4

"Ask Me and I will tell you remarkable secrets
you do not know about things to come."

JEREMIAH 33:3

Get silent before the Lord. Still your mind and quiet your heart. Pray to Him because He is listening to you, and he cares for you.

Are you listening to Him?

We live in a busy world, and it becomes easier everyday to become weighed down with the cares of this world. Use your time wisely to seek His will for your life.

Listen to Him and the way that He communicates with you through scripture, prayer, song, praise, nature, and the counsel of others. Open your Bible and open your heart to His will for your life.

Jennifer

Prayer Request

March 5

> "Then your salvation will come like the dawn, and your wounds will quickly heal. Your godliness will lead you forward and the glory of the Lord will protect you from behind. Then when you call, the Lord will answer. 'Yes, I am here', He will quickly reply."
>
> **ISAIAH 58:8-9**

Friend, I'm encouraging you to Pray!!!! Look around you. What are ways that you can become more aware of God's presence in your life? He is communicating with you if you will only open your eyes, ears, and heart.

Receive God's goodness into your life. His mercies are new every day!

Jennifer

Prayer Request

....

....

March 6

"Stand your ground, putting on the belt of truth and the body armor of God's righteousness."

EPHESIANS 6:14

Have you ever heard the saying, "Put your big girl pants on and deal with it?" If you're facing a challenging situation, this particular saying may or may not apply to you but keep reading nonetheless.

Belts can be too tight. Belts can be too loose. Belts can be stylish yet simple. Belts can be pricey and belts can be inexpensive. Simply put, belts can be very individualized to your specific preferences.

When you put on the "Belt of Truth", you are securing yourself with the word of God. His promises, His Truths, His ways to live your life. When your belt is securely in place, you can walk uprightly, deliberately, and on purpose. You are literally wrapping yourself in the word of God.

So, put your belt on and LIVE your LIFE God's way and with God's truths!

Jennifer

Prayer Request

March 7

"Therefore, put on every piece of God's armor so you will be able to resist the enemy in the time of evil. Then after the battle you will be standing firm."

EPHESIANS 6:13

When you engage in a battle, you need to have some form of protection. Whether it's a helmet, a shield, a gun, a knife, pepper spray, or even a baseball bat. Whatever "it" is, you most likely have "it" in close proximity to you at all times to defend you and your family.

Have you ever considered that the word of God is a protective weapon that you can use to defend yourself against enemy attack? The words you speak become your reality. If you hear something enough, you begin to assert that it is the truth. And that truth becomes YOUR reality on which you live your life.

So, friend, will you believe the lies that the enemy says about you or will you believe the TRUTH? God loves you. He chose you. You were created in His image. You are forgiven. You are His child. You are redeemed. You are righteous. You have a purpose and a calling. You are the apple of His eye.

Let His truth surround you like a shield. You are favored and highly esteemed. You are victorious! Wear those TRUTHS as your armor.

Jennifer

Prayer Request

March 8

> "As for me, I look to the Lord for help. I wait confidently for God to save me, and my God will certainly hear me."
>
> **MICAH 7:7**

When was the last time you talked to the Lord? It doesn't have to be anything elaborate. Are you unsure of where to begin a conversation with Him?

Start with something such as, "I love you, Lord. Thank you for this day. Show me Your will. I trust You to lead me." Watch Him do what only He can do in your life. He is faithful and He is always available to hear you.

Jennifer

Prayer Request

March 9

> "Yes, says the Lord. I will do mighty miracles for you; like those I did when I rescued you from slavery in Egypt."
>
> **MICAH 7:15**

Do you believe that God is still in the miracle working business? Well, He is!

In this world of fabulous light shows at concerts, movies with 3D special effects, and amusement with parks with larger-than-life thrill rides, we may become somewhat numb to the true awesome POWER of God.

Don't confuse the "smoke and mirrors" special effects of this world with GOD's resurrection power.

He is sovereign. He is not dead. He is very much alive! He created the Universe. He is a miracle working God. Talk to Him today - He loves you.

Believe!

Jennifer

Prayer Request

March 10

"For shoes, put on the peace that comes from the Good News so that you will be fully prepared."

EPHESIANS 6:15

Shoes protect our feet and are a necessity in our daily lives. In order to walk or run, our feet need protection from the outside elements.

Just as our shoes are made with leather or some other pliable material, our spiritual "shoes" need to be comprised of God's peace. God's peace surpasses all human understanding and it requires one thing from us as believers and that is trusting Him.

When you know Him through a relationship with Him, you trust Him. And trusting the Lord brings deep, unwavering, unexplainable peace.

When your feet are covered in God's peace, you walk out your faith on a daily basis, leaving footprints of peace in your path. Everywhere you go, I encourage you to go in peace!

Jennifer

Prayer Request

March 11

> "But in that coming day no weapon formed against you will succeed. You will silence every voice raised up to accuse you. These benefits are enjoyed by the servants of the Lord; their vindication will come from Me. I, the Lord, have spoken!"
>
> **ISAIAH 54:17**

Has someone lied to you? Has someone lied about you? Has someone spread gossip about you? Was that person a close friend or family member? Has someone caused or attempted to cause you emotional distress, physical harm, or tried to slander your children's reputations?

So what do we do as Christians?

1. We are directed to pray for our enemies (haters). And know that your ultimate enemy is Satan, and he is a liar and wants you to live in fear.
2. If the situation is very serious and if you need to seek legal action/counseling/assistance of family members/physical protection, I encourage you to do so.
3. Have a TRUSTED group of prayer warriors in agreement with you that no weapon formed against you will prosper.
4. Trust God in this process. He never fails.

Jennifer

Prayer Request

March 12

"For I hold you by your right hand- I, the Lord your God.
And I say to you, 'Don't be afraid. I am here to help you."

ISAIAH 41:13

He will HOLD your right hand. No virus, no plague, no infirmity will stop our Lord from holding your hand. So reach out to Him.

He tells us to not be afraid. So don't be afraid!

And He says that He will GUIDE us. So start letting Him lead you.

Sounds too simple to be true? Think about this fact: He is the Lord and He said it. He doesn't lie. He doesn't change like shifting shadows. He said it, He meant it. Reach out to Him, let Him lead you, and don't be afraid. He's got you and He is here with you.

Jennifer

Prayer Request

March 13

> "Jesus looked at them intently and said, 'Humanly speaking, it is impossible. But not with God. Everything is possible for God.'"
>
> **MARK 10:27**

The disciples had just observed a wealthy man ask Jesus how he could inherit eternal life since he had obeyed all the commandments. When Jesus instructed him to sell all of his possessions and give his money to the poor, he sadly left. Jesus further instructed his disciples that it is difficult for the wealthy to inherit eternal life, specifically, easier for a camel to go through the eye of a needle. But that it was not impossible because everything with God is possible.

I've struggled with this concept of wealth vs. poverty as a sign of "being favored by God" vs. living in poverty as a sign of "being obedient to God." I no longer struggle with it and you'll see why I've changed my mindset if you keep reading.

Here is something that helped me as understanding God's will: Being wealthy can sometimes lead you to become SELF-reliant. Being self-reliant can lead us to becoming egotistical, inflated sense of self-worth, and lack of compassion for others.

Being GOD-reliant acknowledges that all blessings come from Him and treating "my" money as His money. He is the source and He is my provider. Amen!

Jennifer

Prayer Request

. . . .

. . . .

March 14

"For I know the plans I have for you, says the Lord. They are plans for good and not for disaster, to give you a future and a hope. In those days when you pray, I will listen. If you look for ME wholeheartedly, you will find ME. I will be found by you, says the Lord. I will end your captivity and restore your fortunes. I will gather you out of the nations where I sent you and I will bring you home again to your own land."

JEREMIAH 29:11-14

Are you earnestly seeming the Lord and His will for your life? If you are, keep at it! If you're not, why not?

Life WITH God is so much better than life without Him. Invite Jesus Christ into your heart and begin a relationship with Him. Seek Him and watch Him develop you into exactly whom you were created to be for His glory.

Jennifer

Prayer Request

March 15

"Death and life are in the power of the tongue,
and those who love it will eat its fruit."

PROVERBS 8:21

Our mouths can become our greatest asset or our worst foe.

Our words are incredibly powerful. Our words can uplift others and our words can also demean and belittle others. Our words can praise and encourage others. Our words can also spread rumors and tell lies about others. Lies can destroy reputations and families.

What is coming out of your mouth today? I encourage you to speak victory over every situation in your life. Watch how your life changes for the better when your words are used to bring positivity to the world.

Jennifer

Prayer Request

March 16

> "Cast your burdens upon the Lord, and He will sustain you; He shall never permit the righteous to be moved."
>
> **PSALM 55:22**

Often we carry burdens that were never ours to carry. Life can present challenges that we didn't expect and sometimes we place the worry from those situations into "backpacks" that we carry with us wherever we go in life.

Friend, I encourage you to place those concerns at the foot of the cross. Pray and let your Heavenly Father know what or whom is causing you distress and then LET IT GO!

Trust Him to do His best work when you allow Him to take control of all of your fears, worries, concerns, doubts, etc.. He is a good, good Father!

Jennifer

Prayer Request

March 17

> "Trust in the Lord with all of your heart; do not depend on your own understanding. Seek His will in all that you do, and He will show you which path to take."
>
> **PROVERBS 3:5-6**

Frequently we will find ourselves in the position of trying to figure it all out and solve problems that were created at the hands of others. We can be assured that when we trust the Lord, making Him our first priority, truly seeking His will in all of our decisions, He will show up every time to guide us to make the BEST decisions.

If you are dealing with a situation in which you need divine guidance, pray to the Lord for His wisdom. He will direct you as you trust in Him and His will for your life.

Jennifer

Prayer Request

....

....

March 18

"Now, a person who is put in charge as a manager must be faithful."

1 CORINTHIANS 4:2

When someone is faithful, they are trustworthy, dedicated, and committed to the tasks assigned to them. If you are in charge of something, whether it be a family, a business, a financial portfolio, an executive's calendar, or even an event, do it well.

Whatever God has called you to do is considered your "assignment" or "calling" on this earth. We each have unique gifts and abilities that God wants to use through us to bring Him glory. Again, whatever you do, DO IT WELL!

Being faithful produces wonderful results! Adhere to your earthly assignment and you will reap rewards in heaven.

Jennifer

Prayer Request

March 19

"And if God cares so wonderfully for flowers that are here today and thrown into the fire tomorrow, He will certainly care for you. Why do you have so little faith?"

LUKE 12:28

Are you fretting about your future? Sweating over the small stuff and becoming overly anxious about the big stuff?

As I write this, we are in the midst of a Covid pandemic; however, I will choose to not live in constant fear. Whatever you are facing is not too big for God to become involved in it. He is a problem solver and a waymaker. There is a divine order above this chaotic world. And there is ONE God who is in absolute control of the world. He is sovereign.

God is certain. He is stable. He is faithful. He cares for you. Acknowledge Him and trust Him.

Jennifer

Prayer Request

March 20

> "Seek the Kingdom of God above all else, and
> He will give you everything you need."
>
> **MATTHEW 6:33**

SEEK Him. Worship Him. Praise Him. Love Him. Treasure your quiet time with Him. Build a relationship with your Creator. He loves you so.

When you quiet yourself in his presence, you will become aware of how He wants to communicate with you. His voice will bring peace to your soul. His spirit is gentle and kind. He is a perfect gentleman and will wait patiently to be invited into your heart.

He will give you what you need as you continually seek His will for your life.

Jennifer

Prayer Request

....

....

March 21

> "Don't let your hearts be troubled. Trust in God and trust also in Me."
>
> **JOHN 14:1**

What are you worried about right now? What are your thoughts dwelling on? What causes you to have anxious thoughts or sleepless night? Is your mind racing with thoughts of "what if" or "how will this situation work out?"

Friend, we have a God who SEES us. He cares for each one of us. He knows us by name. Reach out to Him today and ask that He help you with whatever you're dealing with/ worried about/ stressed about today? Give it to Him and trust Him to handle it with you.

Jennifer

Prayer Request

March 22

> "Then your salvation will come like the dawn and your wounds will quickly heal. Your godliness will lead you forward and the glory of the Lord will protect you from behind. Then you will call m, the Lord will answer. 'Yes, I am here' He will quickly reply."
>
> **ISAIAH 58:8-9**

He never leaves us. We are not forsaken. His words in scripture remind us of that fact repeatedly. We are loved and we are His children.

The Lord goes before us in every situation. He surrounds us from behind, causing us to not stumble on ourselves. What an awesome God we have, my friends!

Firmly plant yourself in the knowledge that He is the Lord of all! Your focus needs to be on how awesome and powerful He is and how He can heal any situation in your life. He is sovereign.

Let Him heal your heart and your mind. He can do it!

Jennifer

Prayer Request

March 23

> "For I am about to do something new. See, I have already begun! Do you not see it? I will make a pathway through the wilderness. I will create rivers in dry wasteland."
>
> **ISAIAH 43:19**

What are your dreams, hopes, and goals for yourself? For your family? For your business? Are there "dry wasteland" areas of your life such as missed opportunities or relationships that simply faded into oblivion? Are you weary asking/seeking/being persistent in receiving answers to your prayers?

God hears you. God sees you. And He does answer prayers.

Sometimes He answers with a very distinct no.

Sometimes He answers with yes, go ahead!

And sometimes He answers with wait, not yet.

When we are in the wait season, He is developing us and molding us to be able to receive what He is going to give to us.

Just because we ask for it doesn't mean we are ready for it. Like the wonderful Father that He is to us, He always has our best interests at heart. He's not Santa Claus or a Genie in a bottle, He is the Lord. And when the Lord moves on your behalf, nothing can stop Him. Nothing!!

Jennifer

Prayer Request

....

....

March 24

"Take DELIGHT in the Lord, and He will give you the desires of your HEART."

PSALM 37:4

Do you want what God wants for you? Do you ask Him to show you HIS will for your life? Do you spend time with Him daily to learn more about Him? Do you seek His guidance and His wisdom in all areas of your life?

When we spend a significant amount of time with someone, their attitudes, thoughts, and actions "rub off" on us and we become more like them. When you spend more time with the Lord, His attitude, thoughts, and actions become ours. Our hearts become a reflection of His heart. Isn't that so cool?

When our hearts are in alignment with His heart, we can confidently ask for OUR hearts' desires because those exact same desires will be HIS desires.

Jennifer

Prayer Request

March 25

> "Surely the Lord has done great things!
> Don't be afraid, my people. Be glad now and
> rejoice, for the Lord has done great things."
>
> **JOEL 2:21**

Has the Lord done great things in your life? Think about those things He has done for you and REMEMBER them on a daily basis. The more you remember His prior acts, the more you will recall what He has done for you and this will encourage you.

Be grateful. Acknowledge the GIFT-GIVER, not just the gift. He is your source of all things great. He will provide for you and He will make a way for you!

Jennifer

Prayer Request

March 26

"Instead, let the Spirit renew your thoughts and attitudes. Put on your new nature, created to be like God-truly righteous and holy. So stop telling lies. Let us tell our neighbors the truth, for we are all parts of the same body. And don't let anger control you. Don't let the sun go down while you are still angry for anger gives a foothold to the devil."

EPHESIANS 4:23-27

Wow! This scripture is packed with excellent wisdom.

First of all, let the Holy Spirit cleanse you of bad attitudes and negative thought patterns. As you immerse yourself in the Word of God, you are feeding yourself excellent spiritual nutrition. This will create in you a new nature and new you!

Second, tell the truth to yourself, to your neighbors, to everyone. Don't tell lies or spread gossip about others. If you hear a rumor, let it fizzle out and die with you. Your integrity is so valuable.

Third, don't let anger simmer. Pray about whatever is making you angry and reflect on whatever "it" actually is: for example, is it truly someone's actions or is it your reaction?

God is with you and God is for you. He loves you.

Jennifer

Prayer Request

March 27

"Put on salvation as your helmet, and take the sword of the Spirit, which is the word of God."

EPHESIANS 6:17

Are you in a battle right now? A battle for your thoughts, your emotions, your mental stability during this turbulent time? Know this: You have weapons at your disposal.

When you read scripture, you are loading up your arsenal. When you think about/dwell on/meditate on those scripture verses, you're in training for battle. Then, when you speak those scriptures out loud and believe them to be the truth, you have launched an attack!

Put on your Helmet of Salvation, your Shoes of Peace, your Breastplate of Righteousness, your Belt of Truth, and pick up your Sword of Spirit! There is POWER in the Word of God.

Jennifer

Prayer Request

March 28

"The Lord has given me a strong warning not to think like everyone else does. He said, "Don't call anything a conspiracy like they do, and don't live in dread of what frightens them. Make the Lord of Heaven's Armies holy in your life. He is the One you should fear. He is the One who should make you tremble. He will keep you safe."

ISAIAH 8:11-14

Do you respect the Lord? Yes, He is our closest friend but He also is the LORD! Respect His power and sovereignty. Whatever He says He will do, He will do. Period.

When you receive Him into your life as your Savior, I encourage you to invite Him to change your life to reflect what HE wants: His will, His attitude, His character, His loyalty, His compassion, His generosity, His unconditional love, His mercy, His forgiveness, His grace.

As Christians, we strive to reflect the One we love the most.... Jesus Christ.

He is all powerful AND He is gentle. The God who created huge mountains is the same God who created the delicate wings of a butterfly.

He is interested in all the intricate details of your life. Talk to Him, worship Him, build a relationship with Him. It's so worth it!

Jennifer

Prayer Request

March 29

> " Rumors are dainty morsels that
> sink deep into one's heart."
>
> **PROVERBS 18:8**

"Sticks and stones may break my bones but words will never hurt me" is a chant I've heard growing up in Georgia. Have you ever heard it? I don't know if it's just a colloquialism but now that I'm an adult, I realize how it is a completely inaccurate statement of facts.

Sticks, stones, AND words can inflict serious damage to someone. Rumors can affect someone's reputation, career, relationships, and a myriad of other areas, including unnecessary stress. And there are numerous studies linking stress to physical ailments: headaches, ulcers, joint pain, chronic fatigue, etc.

Even if you don't start the rumor, you are still responsible for the negative impact if you spread the rumor. If you've ever started or spread a rumor, let this be an inspiration, NOT condemnation, to make better choices in the future and stop the rumors from flying from your lips.

Here's my advice: let rumors die with you. Don't repeat them, don't start them, pray for the person spreading the rumor, and pray for the person is the subject of the rumor. Watch your life change for the better!

Jennifer

Prayer Request

....

....

March 30

"But you are my witnesses, O Israel!, says the Lord. You are my servant. You have been chosen to know Me, believe in Me, and understand that I alone am God. There is no other God-there never has been and there never will be."

ISAIAH 43:10

Read your Bible, friend! There is one true God and He is sovereign. He is faithful and He is omniscient. And He is OUR FATHER.

Anything that we may be tempted to place above Him is like shifting sands. No social status, no career, no accomplishment, no possession, no relationship should be in the place of the Lord. He wants to have a real relationship with you! Reach out to Him today.

He will not be mocked. He is loving, kind, generous, compassionate, but don't underestimate His awesome power! If He says it, He will do it! His Word will not return void. He is an AWESOME God.

Jennifer

Prayer Request

March 31

> "Before they call I will answer, while they are still speaking I will hear."
>
> **ISAIAH 65:24**

We have a loving God who deeply desires a relationship with us. Just as we listen to our children, God listens and hears us when we cry out to Him. It is such a comfort to me to know that He is interested the big issues of my life as well as the tiny details. He loves me and He loves YOU!

In these uncertain times, know that God still sees you, still hears you, and always loves you. Lean on Him and trust His ways.

Jennifer

Prayer Request

....

....

APRIL

"A hard worker has plenty of food, but
a person who chases fantasies has no sense."

Proverbs 12:11

April 1

"A hard worker has plenty of food, but a person who chases fantasies has no sense."

PROVERBS 12:11

Are you a hard worker? Do you consistently show up for work and give your employer your best? If not, why? Do you play video games instead of working? Do you talk on the phone making personal phone calls on company time?

I encourage you to examine your work ethic. I submit to you that the work we do on this earth is a higher calling and even when the task may seem menial, it is nonetheless important to God. Be a person of excellence. Be a person who seeks to please the Lord at whatever you do, each and every day.

You will be BLESSED for your faithfulness!

Jennifer

Prayer Request

April 2

> "Follow the steps of good men instead and stay on the paths of the righteous. For only the godly will live in the land and those with integrity will remain in it. But the wicked will be removed from the land, and the treacherous will be uprooted."
>
> **PROVERBS 2:20-22**

Do you live with integrity? Do you pursue excellence in your own life? If not, what's stopping you from being your very best self?

Let me encourage you today, friend.

You CAN and you WILL succeed when you partner with the Lord as the leader of your life. Trust Him and allow Him to develop, encourage, and grow you into a person of excellent character. The good work that He started in you He will finish in you.

Jennifer

Prayer Request

April 3

> "Fear of the Lord is the foundation of true knowledge,
> but fools despise wisdom and discipline."
>
> **PROVERBS 1:7**

Do you hate being criticized? Do you abhor having someone redirect you or complain about your work? Your choice of spouse/significant other? Your cooking? Your dreams? Your friendships? Your outfit choice of the day?

Friend, there will always be "haters" in this world. Some people seem to relish being negative or vindictive to others. Don't be one of them. Guard your own mouth and guard your ears.

BUT HEAR THIS: Discipline is very different than hate! There are others who sincerely want you to grow, to develop into whom God called you to be, to rise higher, to seek after EXCELLENCE by following the leading of the Holy Spirit. Allow true wisdom to settle into your heart, your mind, and your spirit.

Jennifer

Prayer Request

April 4

"Come, everyone! Clap your hands! Shout to God with joyful praise! For the Lord Most High is awesome. He is the great King of all the earth."

PSALM 47:1-2

Have you become discouraged in the current political state of the world? While watching the news or reading Facebook posts about politics, do you find yourself becoming exasperated? Does everything just seem unstable?

Run to the Lord with your concerns! Pray for your leaders for wisdom. Respectfully express your opinions/thoughts/ideas to others regarding change in this world. Be kind and be generous to others. And know this fact: THE LORD is the great King of this earth and He is consistent, faithful, and fearless.

Jennifer

Prayer Request

April 5

"Wise words come from the lips of people with understanding, but those lacking sense will be beaten with a rod."

PROVERBS 10:13

While no one wants to be "beaten with a rod" or disgraced in any manner, there are times that discipline is needed to correct our behavior.

Friends, we are living in an age where social media allows people to hide behind slanderous and libelous attacks on the character and reputation of others. This is not fair nor is it just but it IS happening in our world today.

I encourage you to use your words carefully, with thought and humility, before disparaging the reputation of others. Having an opinion is fine but use wisdom in how to offer your opinion to others.

Pray, seek wisdom and direction, and watch how God can use your acts of obedience to Him in positive and honest communication.

The Lord is with each one of us and He shelters His children with peace.

Jennifer

Prayer Request

April 6

"People with integrity walk safely, but those who follow crooked paths will slip and fall."

PROVERBS 10:9

Integrity.

Integrity.

Integrity.

I've heard of you say something 3 times, people will remember it. I urge you to always live a life of INTEGRITY.

What exactly is integrity? When you say what you mean and mean what you say. Have honor, tell the truth, and respect others.

Whether you are at home, at work, at social gatherings, on vacation, at church, at school, be the same person: person who possesses integrity.

Seek wisdom and direction in all that you do.

Jennifer

Prayer Request

April 7

"Hiding hatred makes you a liar; slandering others makes you a fool."

PROVERBS 10:18

Do you have resentment in your heart towards anyone? Before you answer that question, check yourself carefully for any thoughts of negativity towards another person.

Providing forgiveness to someone who has hurt us is not easy, but it IS possible, with the help and guidance of the Holy Spirit. You may think that this is impossible, but it is possible to forgive others with the help of the Holy Spirit.

Ask the Lord to show you the people whom you need to forgive and follow through with forgiving them. It is an act of obedience, not a feeling. It also is a process to make up your mind that you are going to forgive, despite your emotions. You CAN do it, friend!

Jennifer

Prayer Request

April 8

"People who accept discipline are on the pathway to life, but those who ignore correction will go astray."

PROVERBS 10: 17

Discipline is not fun! It is, however, necessary for growth and development. Just as we go to the gym to train and strengthen our bodies, we need to spend time in God's word to strengthen us spiritually. Relationships grow through true quality time and your relationship with the Lord is no different. Spend time with the One you love and the One who loves YOU!

What can you start doing today to make spending time with the Lord a part of your daily routine? Make Him a priority and watch your life improve day by day.

Jennifer

Prayer Request

April 9

> "I have heard all about You, Lord. I am filled with awe by Your amazing works. In this time of our deep need, help us again as You did in years gone by. And in Your anger, remember Your mercy."
>
> **HABAKKUK 3:2**

Despite our unsettled world, I know that God is sovereign. I know that He has a plan and I know that there is ORDER above this chaotic world.

How do I know these facts to be true? I read the Bible and I believe when God says that He is the Creator, He meant it. When He said He was coming back to judge the living and the dead, He meant it. When He is referred to as "just", "kind", "compassionate", "loving", "faithful", "merciful", "redeemer", "tender", "gracious", and "wise", those characteristics are true about Him. And I have a relationship with Him that is the most meaningful relationship of my life.

Do you know Him? He's worth every effort you spend to SEEK Him.

Jennifer

Prayer Request

....

....

April 10

> "Ah, Sovereign Lord, You have made the heavens and the earth by Your great power and outstretched arm. Nothing is too hard for You."
>
> **JEREMIAH 32:17**

Are you dealing with some hard situations in your life right now? Do you think that those hard situations are too hard for the Lord?

Nothing is too hard for the Lord. Absolutely nothing!

I encourage you to "get your praise on" and start thanking God that He goes before you and He is making a way for you! He loves you so! Get your hopes up and believe that you and the Lord are a great team!

TRUST Him and praise Him right now!

Jennifer

Prayer Request

April 11

"You made all the delicate, inner parts of my body and knit me together on my mother's womb. Thank you for making me so wonderfully complex! Your workmanship is marvelous-how well I know it!"

PSALM 139:13-14

You are wonderfully made and created for a purpose. You are a masterpiece and dearly loved by Your Creator. If you're breathing, you still have work left to do on this planet. Get to it!

Let that FACT sink into your spirit today. You're a priceless masterpiece! So loved, so treasured, and so perfectly crafted by the Lord. Realize and recognize that God creates masterpieces and you are a beautiful masterpiece.

Jennifer

Prayer Request

April 12

> "Not only so, but we also glory in our sufferings, because we know that suffering produces perseverance; perseverance, character; and character, hope."
>
> **ROMANS 5:2-4**

Are you naturally a patient person? I know that I am not at all! I want what I want and I want it NOW! Being patient is hard.

But here's what I've learned the older I become: God has His own timetable. His ways are not our ways and His "days" are not our days. He moves and works on His master plan throughout our lives at His pace, not our pace.

Whatever you're dealing with and whatever challenges you face today, know this fact. God loves you and He sees you. He is here for you. He is molding and shaping each one of us into the people He designed us to be for His glory.

He is working ALL things together for our good. Be patient.

Jennifer

Prayer Request

April 13

"So we are always confident, even though we know that as long as we live in these bodies we are not at home with the Lord."

2 CORINTHIANS 5:6

This is not our home. Remember that simple fact. We have not been left on this earth without guidance. We have been provided clear instructions written in the form of the bible. God's word is full of wisdom and peace.

Learn to lean into God's word and His promises for your life. He has a purpose and a plan for your life and He will fulfill it. He Is With You.

Jennifer

Prayer Request

April 14

> "Trust in the Lord and do good, then you will live safely in the land and prosper."
>
> **PSALM 37:3**

My translation of that scripture verse is as follows: Trust the Lord in ALL ways, at ALL times, and in ALL situations in your life.

While it may seem difficult to understand what His plan may be for our lives, I have lived long enough to know this simple fact: HE can be trusted with my life. And He can be trusted with yours, too!

Reach out to Him today and let Him guide you on the best path for your life.

Jennifer

Prayer Request

. . . .

. . . .

April 15

"Take delight in the Lord, and He will give you your heart's desires."

PSALM 37:4

Delighting in the Lord sounds so simple and refreshing, doesn't it? Let's not overcomplicate it, friends! It really is that simple!

Start with opening your eyes in the morning-two gifts from God. Get out of bed, stand up, stretch your legs and arms-more gifts from God. Go to your kitchen, make coffee, decide on your breakfast items from a full pantry-yet another gift from God. Hug your children, pet your dog, get dressed from a full closet of clothes, drive your car, go to your job: all are gifts from God. You understand the idea now?

Be THANKFUL for every single gift in your life. You'll start delighting in your day and your walk with the Lord in ways you could never imagine! Ask Him how you can bless others!

Jennifer

Prayer Request

....

....

April 16

"Your word is a lamp to my feet and a light to my path."

PSALM 119:105

How does the Lord speak to us? One powerful way is through His word, the holy scriptures in the bible. When we read the Bible, we are reading His instruction manual for life. We receive wisdom and direction from the Bible and through prayer with God.

The Bible is full of life-changing promises, to include eternal salvation. What He says, He means. His word will not return void! If you need peace, wisdom, clarity, direction, guidance, mercy, grace, compassion, or healing, read your Bible. If you aren't reading your Bible, what are you reading or watching on a daily basis? I encourage you to pick up your Bible today and allow the word of God to fill your mind and soul.

Jennifer

Prayer Request

April 17

> "But this is the new covenant I will make with
> the people of Israel on that day", says the Lord,
> " I will put my instructions deep within them
> and I will write them on their hearts. I will be
> their God and they will be my people."
>
> **JEREMIAH 31:33**

Is your heart stony and stubborn? How about allowing the Lord to give you a heart transplant?

Allow Him to work in your heart today and remove the callouses on your heart. Invite Him into your life to become Lord of your life. He will soften that hardened heart and you will never be the same again. Trust Him to do a good work in you!

Jennifer

Prayer Request

....

....

April 18

> "What a wildly wonderful world, God! You made it all, with Wisdom at your side, made earth overflow with your wonderful creations!"
>
> **PSALM 104:24**

Look UP in the sky! Look around you at the beautiful world! Look down at the grass, flowers, sand, dirt, snow, wherever you are and realize that God made it all. All of it is His creation!

Friend, if He made this entire Universe with all of its splendor and intricate detail, don't you know that He created YOU for a unique purpose? You are a masterpiece and ask the Lord to show you His plan for your life! You are a child of the King!

Jennifer

Prayer Request

April 19

> "No, O People, the Lord has told you what is good
> and this is what He requires of you: to do what is right,
> to love mercy, and to walk humbly with your God."
>
> **MICAH 6:8**

I encourage you to read that scripture verse again slowly. Maybe even a second time.

This scripture verse is a favorite verse of one of my personal heroes and I understand why it is his favorite. As a well respected leader in our community, he completely embodies mercy and justice and is a very humble person.

Yet even though I admire these qualities in my long time friend, I must continue to direct my eyes on Jesus, who truly exemplified each one of these traits in every aspect of His time on this earth. Jesus was and still is full of mercy and humility.

Friend, people will fail us and disappoint us because no one is perfect. Turn your eyes to the One who never will fail you. He is always present, always consistent, and always here for you!

Jennifer

Prayer Request

April 20

"And I will give you a new heart, and I will put a new spirit in you. I will take out your stony, stubborn heart and give you a tender, responsive heart."

EZEKIEL 36:26

Are you in need of a heart transplant today? Let the Lord remove your stubborn heart and replace it with a tender, responsive heart. You may wonder exactly how that would occur and my response is to spend TIME with the Lord.

Seek Him to KNOW Him. Once you begin spending time with Him through reading His word, praying to Him, and meditating on His promises, you'll begin to fill that void in your heart.

You are His child and He loves you.

Jennifer

Prayer Request

April 21

> "They entered the house and saw the child with His mother, Mary, and they bowed down and worshipped Him. Then they opened their treasure chests and gave Him gifts of gold, frankincense, and myrrh."
>
> **MATTHEW 2:11-12**

The three wise men were in awe of Jesus. They believed in Him and even asserted by their actions that He was, in fact, the Messiah. They traveled great distances to see Him, to humble themselves before Him, and to present valuable gifts to Him.

Let me ask you: What distance are you willing to travel for Jesus? Are you willing to humble yourself before Him? And what "gifts" can you present to Him?

Your gift can be using your God-given talents, fully developing them and using them for His glory. Your gift could be spending time in His word, treasuring His instructions to us as Believers. Your gift may be encouraging others to stand strong in the face of illness or helping someone in financial crisis.

Learn from the wise men. Seek the Lord wholeheartedly and USE your GIFTS for God!

Jennifer

Prayer Request

April 22

"Your love for one another will prove to the world that you are My disciples."

JOHN 13:35

Do you love others? Truly love them, hold them in high regard, esteem them, care for them, pray for them, delight in their triumphs, and mourn with them when they face disappointments? If you do, that is excellent and you will be grateful when others do this for you, too.

If you do not love others, ask the Lord for His joy and love to fill your heart to overflowing capacity. He will love you and His love will fill your heart to the point that you truly desire to show love to others.

As believers, we are commanded to love one another. Jesus first loved us.

Love is a call to action! Respond to the call to love others and you will never regret it.

Jennifer

Prayer Request

April 23

> "This is what the Lord of Heaven's Armies says: All this may seem impossible to you now, a small remnant of God's people. But is it impossible for Me? says the Lord of Heaven's Armies."
>
> **ZECHARIAH 8:7**

This small remnant of God's people were individuals who had returned from Babylon to rebuild Jerusalem and the Temple. When facing an enormous task, they were tempted to become discouraged.

Are you facing a seemingly "impossible" situation today? Do you feel outnumbered, overwhelmed, or exhausted? Friend, the same God who encouraged these exiles in Jerusalem still sits on the throne today. He doesn't change and He cannot lie. If He said it, He meant it. Nothing is impossible for Him.

HE IS OUR GOD and He fights for us!

Start worshipping and quit worrying!

Jennifer

Prayer Request

April 24

"But now I will not treat the remnant of my people as I treated them before; says the Lord of Heaven's Armies. For I am planting seeds of peace and prosperity among you. The grapevines will be heavy with fruit. The earth will produce its crops, and the heavens will release the dew. Once more I will cause the remnant in Judah and Israel to inherit these blessings."

ZECHARIAH 8: 12-12

Are you a patient person? If so, that is a wonderful quality. I am not naturally a patient person but I have begun to learn how many blessings come from being patient! Whether it's dealing with paying off debt, managing finances, developing healthy eating habits, or simply slowing down to enjoy the company of a friend, being patient has great rewards.

Our God is a patient God. Instead of focusing on what you don't have, try to praise Him for what you do have and thank Him for what's on the way! When God decides it is time to release His blessings, watch out! He is a good God and His timing is not our timing. Trust Him. He knows best!

Jennifer

Prayer Request

April 25

"For the Lord always keeps His promises;
He is gracious in all He does."

PSALM 145: 13

Has someone failed to keep a promise to you? Are you hurting today because of a broken relationship? Did someone lie about you, spread gossip about you, or take something/someone from you? Has someone violated your trust, said cruel things to you or about you? Have you felt abandoned, rejected, ignored?

Friend, this world can be tough at times but know this FACT: God is faithful. He cannot lie. God is 100 percent trustworthy!

He is loyal, kind, generous, forgiving, compassionate, merciful, and always rooting for you and your best interests! He is solid as a rock, a firm foundation, and the best friend you will ever have-I promise!

Jennifer

Prayer Request

....

....

April 26

> "And you will know the truth and
> the truth will set you free."
>
> **JOHN 8:32**

Jesus spoke those words to His believers and they questioned what He meant by it since they were not slaves to anyone. Jesus advised them that the freedom He spoke of was in regards to being a slave to sin. We are all tempted and we all are sinners.

Friends, the TRUTH of God's love and redemption truly will set you free. I promise!

Ask Him into your heart and watch what He will do as you honor Him with your life. Lean into His word and His guidance will show you the way to live your best life.

Jennifer

Prayer Request

April 27

"...See, I have written your name on the palms of My hands."

ISAIAH 49:16

Until a few years ago, I had a habit of writing on my hands anything urgent or important I needed to remember. I knew if it was written on my hands, I would continually see it and it would remind me of whatever it was I needed to do.

Isn't it a comfort to know that YOUR NAME is written on the palms of our Lord? YOUR NAME is continually on His mind!

The Lord comforts His people and consoles the broken-hearted. Are you feeling pain, disappointment, discouragement, or depression today?

Seek Him. Spend time with Him. Trust Him to guide you in every single area of your life. The more time you spend with Him, the more He fills us with His likeness: mercy, goodness, power, love, hope, joy, faith, kindness, peace, encouragement, abundance, strength, gentleness, patience, redemption, trustworthiness, and His beautiful grace.

Spend some time today with our Savior.

Jennifer

Prayer Request

April 28

"Don't be afraid! I am the First and the Last. I am the Living One. I died but look-I am living forever and ever! And I hold the keys of death and the grace."

REVELATION 1:17

When someone wants to get your attention, do they ever have to repeat themselves? When someone repeats themselves, it typically means that you need to pay close attention to whatever they are trying to tell you.

Do not be afraid. Do not fear. Have no fear. Fear not and Be courageous. The Lord instructs us repeatedly in the Bible to NOT be afraid.

So why are you afraid? The Creator of the Universe has got your back!

Jennifer

Prayer Request

April 29

> "Because of Christ and our faith in Him, we can now come boldly and confidentially into God's presence."
>
> **EPHESIANS 3:12**

Don't be meek and mild with the Lord! SEEK Him through prayer. PRAISE Him for who He is and express your love to Him through your obedience to His word.

I've heard people ask, "Why should I pray because God already knows what I need?" but I still urge you to pray to Him, seek Him, and build a relationship with Him. Doesn't it soften your heart when your own children come to you for guidance and direction?

The Lord is sovereign and He does already know what you need; however, He desires a personal relationship with you. Come with confidence to seek God and His will for your life.

Jennifer

Prayer Request

....

....

April 30

"Let your roots grow down into Him, and let your lives be built on Him. Then your faith will grow strong in the truth you were taught, and you will overflow with thankfulness."

COLOSSIANS 2:7

When you plant a seed, it doesn't sprout overnight. It takes time for it to blossom and grow into what it was intended to be: a flower, a tree, a vegetable, a fruit, etc.

In a similar way, when we accepted the Lord into our lives, a seed of faith was planted in our hearts. As we mature and develop as Christians, our faith grows and blossoms into a beautiful relationship.

Your faith "seed" is watered by reading God's word, reflecting on how it applies to your life, and developed through daily application of Christian principles. You are growing each day!

Jennifer

Prayer Request

MAY

"The Lord detests dishonest scales, but accurate weights find favor with Him."

Proverbs 11:1

May 1

"The Lord detests dishonest scales, but accurate weights find favor with Him."

PROVERBS 11:1

Be honest. I repeat, BE HONEST. In all of your dealings with all people. Be honest.

If you've been dishonest in the past, ask forgiveness and make it right. Repay the money, write the letter, make the phone call, pay the debt, do whatever is needed to mend the wrong you caused to another person.

If you're currently being dishonest, stop it. Friend, stop it now!

If you're questioning if you've been dishonest in a particular situation, ask God to show you where you've been dishonest and how to correct that behavior. Seek forgiveness and make it right with whomever you've been dishonest.

Jennifer

Prayer Request

May 2

"The highest angelic powers stand in awe of God. He is far more awesome than those who surround His throne."

PSALM 89:7

Do you believe in angels? Have you ever noticed the amount of jewelry, movies, greeting cards, costumes, books, stickers, songs, blankets, photos, yard art, or other collectibles that have been made with an image or reference to angels?

Angels tend to summon up general feelings of goodwill towards others. Yes, angelic beings do exist but even they stand in awe of our Lord!

HE is worthy of praise and honor! Angels stand in AWE of Him. We should, too.

Jennifer

Prayer Request

May 3

> "The Lord your God is with you; the Mighty Warrior who saves; He will take great delight in you; in His love He will no longer rebuke you but will rejoice over you with singing."
>
> **ZEPHANIAH 3:17**

This scripture verse always brings a huge smile to my face. The simple thought that the Lord takes great delight in me to the point of singing over me makes me truly happy. He loves each one of us as His individual masterpiece. That's YOU and that's ME.

He is also our Mighty Warrior. What problem or situation are you facing today that you need to give to Him to fight on your behalf? I encourage you to LET IT GO and give it to Him. Wherever He leads you, trust Him. He's got you and He's got me.

Have a wonderful day, my sweet friend!

Jennifer

Prayer Request

....

....

May 4

> "But when you pray, go away by yourself, shut the door behind you, and pray to your Father in private. Then your Father, who sees everything, will reward you."
>
> **MATTHEW 6:6**

How frequently do you pray? Where do you pray? When do you pray? Why do you pray?

Prayer is simply communicating with our Creator. Communication is necessary for relationships to grow and blossom.

When someone is in close relationship with us, it is natural to tell them everything about ourselves: hopes, desires, dreams, failures, mistakes, wonderful news and bad news. Especially when it is your best friend or closest ally.

If you're not close to God, Start praying..... You moved, He didn't! Draw near to Him in prayer. He is always there for you.

Jennifer

Prayer Request

May 5

"Oh Magnify the Lord with me, and let us exalt His name together."

PSALM 34:3

When a friend compliments you on your attire, how does that make you feel? If a co-worker tells you that you're awesome, don't you just glow? If your spouse lets you know that you're attractive, don't you become radiant? Praise is always appreciated.

Praises bring honor to the Lord. When was the last time you praised the Lord? He DESERVES it and mighty is His name. Start listing the times He's rescued you from situations, loved you when you felt unlovable, forgiven you for terrible acts you committed, been gentle with you when you've been harsh with someone, defended you when you've been innocent, shielded you from disaster, healed you from disease, and the list continues into eternity.

HE doesn't change. He is the Creator. He is unshakable and unstoppable in His love for YOU. Praise Him!

Jennifer

Prayer Request

May 6

> ".... What's more, I am with you, and I will protect you wherever you go. One day I will bring you back to this land. I will not leave you until I have finished giving you everything I have promised you."
>
> **GENESIS 28:15**

How comforting to know that God never leaves us. That is a promise from God and His promises are the truth.

He is the God who stays with us at all times and in all circumstances. There is a popular contemporary Christian song entitled, "The God Who Stays" by Matthew West and the words truly resonate with me. The simple but powerful lyrics discuss how God is the God who stays, how He is the God who runs in our direction when the whole world walks away. He runs in our direction!

Friend, if you are in the midst of any type of a struggle, whether it is emotional, spiritual, financial, physical, and/or relational, I strongly encourage you to pick up your bible and read it. God doesn't leave you to wander through this world by yourself. He is with you. He is the God who stays, the God who runs in your direction, and the God who loves you so!

Jennifer

Prayer Request

May 7

"Delight yourself in the Lord and He will give you the desires of your heart."

PSALM 37:4

Today is a special day for me. It's my 50th birthday! So please indulge me while I explain how this scripture is applicable to all believers everywhere on this planet.

When we learn to truly TRUST the Lord with our whole heart, we are being refined and molded in His image. And as believers, by placing our total TRUST in Him and acknowledging that His plan for our lives is the BEST plan, we know that He has us in the palm of His hands.

That simple, but powerful act of TRUSTING the Lord is an act of obedience and total devotion to Him. Literally, it is the surrendering of our own selfish desires to His plan and His will for our lives. And from that act of surrendering our hearts to Him, our hearts' desires will come into alignment with the Lord's desires for our lives.

Keep reading, friend.

Surrender your whole heart to the Lord.

Jennifer

Prayer Request

May 8

> "You are worthy, O Lord our God, to receive glory and honor and power. For You created all things, and they exist because you created what you pleased."
>
> **REVELATION 4:11**

Revelation is a book in the Bible that the beloved apostle John wrote as a book of hope, but also as a warning. It is a source of HOPE to believers and warning to those who align themselves with evil.

Do you know that you are loved? Do you know that you were uniquely designed for a purpose? Do you know that you are valuable? Do you know that you have HOPE?

When you breathe your final breath, it's not the end! It's just the beginning! Where do you want to spend eternity? Talk to the Lord through prayer today, ask Him to forgive your sins and dwell in your heart forever.

Jennifer

Prayer Request

May 9

> "O Lord God of Heaven's Armies! Where is anyone as mighty as You, O Lord? You are entirely faithful."
>
> **PSALM 89:8**

This scripture verse portrays the Lord as mighty and the leader of the heaven's armies. Mighty typically equals great strength. And He surely is the source of great strength, ready to defend and protect us at all times.

But did you read the reference to His "faithfulness" as our Lord? I don't know that I would have used that description of "faithful" immediately after referring Him as a "warrior", but it actually makes perfect sense.

Think about it...Who else do you want fighting your battles? I associate faithfulness with consistency, diligence, and steadfastness. That's exactly who our Lord is for us: FAITHFUL in battling for us!

Jennifer

Prayer Request

....

....

May 10

"Jesus replied to Simon (Peter), 'Don't be afraid! From now on you'll be fishing for people!' And as soon as they landed, they left everything behind and followed Jesus."

LUKE 5:10-11

Prior to this miracle, Simon (Peter) and his crew had fished all night and caught nothing. They arrived at the shoreline and Jesus stepped onto their boat. Jesus subsequently used their boat as a platform to sit on and address and teach the crowds that were surrounding them on the shore. It was after Jesus used their boat as a platform that He blessed them with an overflow of fish.

Friend, are you allowing Jesus to use your business as a platform to teach the Gospel? Have you invited Him into every situation you encounter? Does your work reflect your love for the Lord? You have been given special gifts and abilities-use them wisely!

Jesus doesn't want to only be involved in your life on Sundays at church! Get Him out of that box you've placed Him into and invite Him into your entire week. Yes, that includes your daily routine, too.

Jennifer

Prayer Request

May 11

"In view of all this, make every effort to respond to God's promises. Supplement your faith with a generous provision of moral excellence, and moral excellence with knowledge, and knowledge with self-control, and self-control with patient endurance, and patient endurance with godliness, and godliness with brotherly affection, and brotherly affection with love for everyone."

2 PETER 1: 5-7

Every day is a journey! Hopefully, we are growing closer in our relationship with the Lord on a daily basis. Like all relationships, spending time and communicating with the one you love is vital to growth.

Is your relationship with Jesus your number one priority? Please re-read that question. Only you can answer it.

As a relationship grows and develops into something beautiful, TRUST is needed at all times and in all situations. The Lord will never fail you. Again, He will never fail you.

People are imperfect. No matter how hard we try, we are not perfect. We all will fail at our feeble attempts to make one another happy all the time.

Why not place your relationship priorities in alignment with God's priorities: God first, people second. That's His way and that's the BEST way!

Jennifer

Prayer Request

May 12

"No one who performs a miracle in My name will soon be able to speak evil of Me. Anyone who is not against us if for us. If anyone gives you even a cup of water because you belong to the Messiah, I tell you the truth, that person will surely be rewarded."

MARK 9:40-41

Are you believing for a miracle in your own life? A healing, a promotion, a relationship to be restored, a financial blessing?

Friend, today is the day and today is the time for you to become someone else's miracle! Look around you and see who God placed in your life. Who needs your quality time and listening ear? Who needs a visit from you? Who needs some encouragement? Who needs a ride to work or some help moving into their new home? Who needs a financial gift? Go do it. Bless someone else today!

Jennifer

Prayer Request

May 13

> "May the Lord continually bless you from Zion. May you see Jerusalem prosper as long as you live. May you live to enjoy grandchildren. May Israel have peace."
>
> **PSALM 128: 5-6**

If I could pick any ONE blessing that comes from being a Christian, I would have to say it is the PEACE of God. I love knowing that my eternity is secure with Him and that He is always with me. This world can be chaotic but He never leaves me.

When you accept Jesus into your heart, your eternity is securely fastened with Him. But that's not the end of what happens! He doesn't leave us stranded on earth without His heavenly resources. He is WITH us! He's the best friend you could ever want and the best friend you will ever need in your life.

Are you anxious? Are you confused, frightened, feeling vulnerable? Submit your emotions to the Lord and lean on Him. He cares for you.

Jennifer

Prayer Request

. . . .

. . . .

May 14

"He has showered His kindness on us, along with all wisdom and understanding."

EPHESIANS 1:7

When Paul wrote this letter to the Ephesians, he was under house arrest in Rome. At other times throughout his life, Paul was arrested and placed in jail. In ancient times, jails were truly in deplorable conditions, such as no running water, no ventilation for fresh air, dirt/clay/stone floors, the unwelcome presence of rodents and bugs, sparse food, etc.

Paul continued to be faithful in writing letters to encourage and edify the various churches located in cities such as Corinth and Ephesus. He was committed to spreading the Gospel. And he praised God throughout his circumstances, whether he was free or incarcerated.

Friend, read that scripture listed above again! Paul, despite his circumstances, refers to the Lord as "showering kindness" and granting "wisdom and understanding." Wow! What a wonderful example for all of us.

Gratitude at its very best.

Jennifer

Prayer Request

May 15

"Darkness as black as night covers all the nations of the earth, but the glory of the Lord rises and appears over you."

ISAIAH 60:2

Our world is becoming darker and this has affected so many aspects of our lives. Pandemics, strange weather conditions, and financial crisis are just a few of the areas of concern which cause unnecessary anxiety to family members, business owners, first responders, college graduates, and the elderly in nursing homes. Everyone everywhere has been affected by multiple issues.

The Lord sees you. The Lord cares about you. And He is with you. Stay safe, my friend, but most importantly, stay CONNECTED to your Creator!

Jennifer

Prayer Request

....

....

May 16

> "To all who mourn in Israel, He will give a crown of beauty for ashes, a joyous blessing instead of mourning, festive praise instead of despair. In their righteousness, they will be like great oaks that the Lord has planted for His glory."
>
> **ISAIAH 61:3**

Friend, our compassionate God SEES you!

Our mighty God HEARS your prayers.

Our majestic God LOVES you.

Whatever challenges or obstacles you've endured will be ultimately used for His glory! He knows every single detail of your life. Nothing is too difficult for Him. Nothing!

He's got you!

Jennifer

Prayer Request

May 17

> "This is what the Sovereign Lord says: 'Look! I am going to put breath into you and make you live again! I will put flesh and muscles on you and cover you with skin. I will put breath into you, and you will come to life. Then you will know that I am the Lord."
>
> **EZEKIEL 37:5-6**

Ezekiel's vision of the valley of dry bones illustrated a new Israel, restored physically and spiritually. The promises from chapter 36 of a new heart, clean, filled with the Spirit of God, returning home to their own land were not yet fulfilled. But hope was restored to Ezekiel through the vision of what God can do with seemingly dead situations.

Friend, what situations appear to be lifeless to you today? I encourage you to invite the Lord into that situation and watch what He can do!

Jennifer

Prayer Request

....

....

May 18

"My thoughts are nothing like your thoughts, says the Lord. And My ways are far beyond anything you could imagine."

ISAIAH 55:8

It's easy to become frustrated or irritated at the little things in life. You've probably heard the expression, "Don't sweat the small stuff" and agreed with it in theory but putting it into daily practice can become quite a challenge.

Friend, when God said that His thoughts are not our thoughts, He absolutely meant it. His ways are higher and His ways are better. Trust Him in every area of your life and know that He has a plan. He can be trusted to complete the good work He started in you.

Jennifer

Prayer Request

May 19

> "To those who use well what they are given, even more will be given, and they will have an abundance. But those who do nothing, even what little they have will be taken away."
>
> **MATTHEW 25:14**

What GIFTS has the Lord bestowed upon you?

Are your parents still alive? Call or visit them, assist them with household chores.

Are you married? Be faithful to your spouse, respect them, love and cherish them.

Are you a parent? Provide for your children, raise them with kindness and teach them humility.

Are you employed? Show your employer honor and respect, work hard at your job.

Do you have a home? Pay your bills, save for the future, and take care of your earthly possessions.

Are you healthy? Take care of your body: eat well, exercise, stay up to date on visits to your physician, and get proper rest.

Whatever GIFTS the Lord has bestowed upon you, take care of them.

Jennifer

Prayer Request

. . . .

. . . .

May 20

"Love your enemies! Do good to them. Lend to them without expecting to be repaid. Then your reward from heaven will be very great, and you will truly be acting as children of the Most High, for He is kind to those who are unthankful and wicked."

LUKE 6:35

The Lord is kind and merciful to all. Praying for our enemies and seeking opportunities to bless them will be seen by our Creator. Loving God to the point of being genuinely kind to our enemies is goal worthy!

"Live your life on your own terms" is something our society holds in high regard. As Christians, we are called to live life on HIS terms: loving Him in first place and loving people in second place.

Jennifer

Prayer Request

May 21

"...Oh, that you would choose life, so that you and your descendants might live!"

DEUTERONOMY 30:19

When we make the choice to love God first, completely committing ourselves to His will, acknowledging His sovereignty and obeying Him, then we have the key to life. It sounds so simple, doesn't it?

Ask God to help re-arrange your priorities to put Him in first place in your life. His way is the best way to live and His word is a lamp to your path. When you dwell on His promises, He will fill your life with peace, joy, and wisdom.

Choose the path to LIFE in Christ!

Jennifer

Prayer Request

May 22

> "For I can do everything through
> Christ, who gives me strength!"
>
> **PHILIPPIANS 4:13**

Jesus Christ died on the cross for all of our sins. He loves each one of us unconditionally. He rose from the dead and He is ALIVE!

As believers, we know that His resurrection power is at work within each of us. There is nothing that is impossible for Christ. If you need wisdom, ask Him. If you need peace, ask Him. If you need strength, ask Him. If you need healing, ask Him.

Let HIM be your guide and your source of true strength!

Jennifer

Prayer Request

May 23

> "Now this is the confidence that we have in Him, that if we ask anything according to His will, He hears us. And if we know that He hears us, whatever we ask, we know that we have the petitions that we have asked of Him."
>
> **1 JOHN 5:14-15**

Have you ever been talking to someone and it appears as if they are distracted? Perhaps they are glancing down at their phone/watch or looking around the room during the conversation? Or perhaps they interrupt you or seem to want to share their story before you've finished yours? Annoying, isn't it?

I've been guilty of all of the above actions of a distracted listener. And I've also been the recipient of being in a conversation with a distracted listener. It's rude and it's also very human.

It encourages me to know that every single time that I lift my voice in praise, my hands in prayer, and/or my heart's petitions to the Lord, HE HEARS and HE SEES me. And He sees and hears you, too. Every single time.

Jennifer

Prayer Request

....

....

May 24

"Never let loyalty and kindness leave you! Tie them around your neck as a reminder. Write them deep within your heart. Then you will find favor with both God and people, and you will earn a good reputation."

PROVERBS 3:3-4

Your circle of friends should be so loyal to you that when you leave the room you don't become the topic of their conversation. And visa versa.

Be a loyal person. It is scriptural (see above).

Be a kind person. It is scriptural (see above).

Being loyal and being kind are also examples of using good manners. Try it and watch how your life improves in every relationship.

Jennifer

Prayer Request

May 25

"For I know the plans I have for you," says the Lord. "They are plans for good and not for disaster, to give you a future and a hope. In those days when you pray, I will listen. If you look for me wholeheartedly, you will find me. I will be found by you," says the Lord. "I will end your captivity and restore your fortunes. I will gather you out of the nations where I sent you and will bring you home again to your own land."

JEREMIAH 29:11

What God promises, He will fulfill. What promises are you standing on today, friend? Are you dwelling on the negative circumstances in your life or are you focusing on the positive future that God promises you in scripture?

If He said it, He will do it. Watch Him! He is faithful and He is trustworthy. He will guide you as you trust Him.

Jennifer

Prayer Request

....

....

May 26

"Light is sweet; how pleasant to see a new day dawning."

ECCLESIASTES 11:7

Each day is a new beginning!

Every 24 hours we start a new day, with new opportunities, and new grace. And the transition into the new day begins when you "open your eyes" (physically and spiritually) to see the Lord's fresh anointing, peace, and blessings on YOU!

When your day begins with praise and thanksgiving, your heart is filled with gratitude and peace. When your heart is filled with gratitude and peace, your conduct responds accordingly.

Enjoy your new day!

Jennifer

Prayer Request

May 27

> "Learn to do good. Seek justice. Help the oppressed. Defend the cause of the orphans. Fight for the rights of widows."
>
> **ISAIAH 1:17**

As Christians, we are called to LOVE others, even our enemies. While we may find their actions unlikeable, we are still called to love them as a fellow human being. When we are filled with the love of Christ, our cup overflows with that love to others.

Having said that, being a Christian does not mean that we become doormats. We can have different opinions, different tastes, different interests, different friends, different talents and unique skills.

We are called to love others and to live at peace; however, we are to conduct ourselves according to biblical truths: defend our faith, be honest, love others, seek justice, have patience, be kind, show generosity, and remember who we serve, The Lord!

Jennifer

Prayer Request

....

....

May 28

> "Do not be deceived. Bad company corrupts good morals."
>
> **1 CORINTHIANS 15:33**

With whom do you spend your time?

Your time is a valuable commodity! Spend it in the presence of quality individuals.

I encourage you to examine your closest relationships. As believers, we are called to love others. We are also instructed to live at peace with everyone whenever it is possible.

However, if the people in your closest circle are constantly filled with hate, strife, jealousy, pettiness, gossip, or negativity, pay close attention to what your heart is telling you. Observe with your eyes, ears, heart, and discern accordingly.

Love them, pray for them, and encourage them to be filled with the peace and joy of Christ. But their place is not in your closest circle of friends. Again, love them, pray for them, and encourage them.

Pray for God to guide and direct you as to those whom need to be in your closest circle of friends. Stay close to those who encourage, nurture, edify, love, pray with you and for you.

Jennifer

Prayer Request

....

....

May 29

"Those who listen to instruction will prosper;
those who trust in the Lord will be joyful."

PSALM 16:20

Do you know the difference between challenging someone vs. cursing someone?

When we challenge someone to come up higher, we are encouraging them to grow in a certain area. For instance, you can present a challenge to someone to work out consistently for 90 days or to complete a 6 week bible study. You check in with that person on a regular basis for accountability and to provide support to them. You speak LIFE into that person and are excited to watch them prosper!

When you curse someone, you genuinely expect the worst in someone. You belittle them and expect them to fail every time in every situation. You expect negativity in their lives and you believe that their negative behaviors will continue without any hope. If you are someone who is doing this to someone else, especially to someone in your own family, please STOP! It's not too late to change that behavior.

Speak LIFE into your conversations, filling your conversations with love, support, and encouragement.

Read the word of God. He is the true source of hope, love, peace, joy, wisdom, and faith.

Jennifer

Prayer Request

May 30

"Lord, my God, I cried to You for help,
and You restored my health."

PSALM 30:2

Are you aware that God hears your prayers? Every single prayer. God answers prayers. Every single prayer.

God answers prayers with His master plan always in motion. His thoughts are not our thoughts and His ways are not our ways.

There is a saying, "His answers to prayers are Yes, No, and Wait." The longer I am alive on this planet, the more I agree with that statement and see it to be true in my own life.

Friend, God hears every one of your prayers. His silence doesn't indicate that your prayers are falling on deaf ears. Remember that God has a master plan and everything is subject to His divine authority. Trust Him and trust His timing.

Jennifer

Prayer Request

May 31

> "Dear friends, let us continue to love one another, for love comes from God. Anyone who loves is a child of God and knows God."
>
> **1 JOHN 4:7**

On Memorial Day and other military holidays, we honor those who sacrificed their lives for our freedom. It is a time to reflect and express our gratitude for the unselfish actions of those who have protected our liberty, to the expense of their own lives. Their heroic actions of placing our lives above their own is an unselfish act of love. We are grateful.

Having a heart of gratitude is also having a heart of love. What is love? How is love shown to others? Do you truly love your family and your friends? Loving someone doesn't mean that you will always agree with them nor does it mean that you'll always have the same thoughts/attitudes/beliefs.

Apply the above-stated scripture to your own life and watch how your life is enhanced. God is LOVE and if you truly love the Lord, you will LOVE others!

Jennifer

Prayer Request

....

....

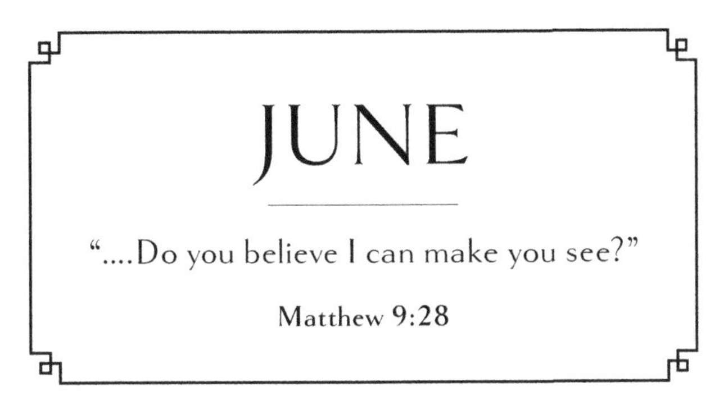

JUNE

"....Do you believe I can make you see?"

Matthew 9:28

June 1

"....Do you believe I can make you see?"

MATTHEW 9:28

Jesus was a healer. This particular scripture occurred immediately after Jesus healed the Synagogue Leader's little girl. The crowds went from mocking Him to spreading news of the miracle throughout the entire countryside.

When Jesus left the little girl's home, He was followed by two blind men, who cried out to Him to have mercy on them. Jesus could've just quietly and quickly healed them without any words but He stopped and asked them if they BELIEVED He could do it.

Their actions (following Him) combined with their spoken words (cries for mercy) combined with their FAITH (they responded yes that they believed) got His attention!

Friend, what do you desperately need today? Have you made your specific request known to the Lord? Have you put faith-filled actions behind it? And do you BELIEVE He can do the impossible? Lean into God. Let Him be your source of strength.

Jennifer

Prayer Request

....

....

June 2

> "Pay careful attention to your own work, for then you will get the satisfaction of a job well done, and you won't need to compare yourself to anyone else. For we are each responsible for our own conduct."
>
> **GALATIANS 6:4-5**

I think I could read that verse a hundred times and it would still resonate with me. I love it and here's why: it reminds me who is truly in charge of my life.

If you are a business owner, I understand the challenges you face on a daily basis of juggling the performance of your own job, managing budgets, plan for retirement, generating revenue, hiring/supervising employees, office supplies, handling clients and their needs, maintaining the office building, advertising, and still attempting to have a life outside of work. It isn't easy! And to top it off, we live in a society of constant comparison to others.

Read that scripture again. Perform your job to the very best of your ability, trust God, and don't compare yourself to anyone else.

Jennifer

Prayer Request

June 3

"So let's not get tired of doing what is good.
At just the right time we will reap a harvest of
blessing if we don't give up. Therefore, whenever
we have the opportunity, we should do good to
everyone-especially to those in the family of faith."

GALATIANS 6:9-10

How many times in your life have you given up on something? It could be a plan, a business venture, dream, a task, a project, or even a relationship? Did you regret it? Was the Lord guiding your decision to end it?

Yes, there are situations where it is appropriate to sever ties with someone or no longer pursue a particular dream. However, there are also some difficult situations where we simply need to dig our heels in and stick with it, too. Don't get tired of doing good.

Trust God to show you when and how to handle those difficult or challenging situations in your life. It could be time to sever ties and move on BUT it could also be time to stay put right where you are and keep chugging full steam ahead, doing good and not growing weary.

Jennifer

Prayer Request

....

....

June 4

"... always seek to do good to each other and everyone else."

1 THESSALONIANS 5:15

Being good to someone you love is easy, isn't it? What about being good to people who annoy you? What about being good to someone who lies about you, gossips about you or your loved ones, or someone who steals from you?

Friend, being good to others is an action that stems from your HEART. When are hearts are right with God, we WANT to be good to others.

I encourage you to give your heart to Jesus. Allow Him to completely accept and love you just as you are right now!

Little by little, day by day, month by month, year by year, His love transforms us into His image of compassion, mercy, faith, generosity, obedience, humility, and most importantly, LOVE.

He FIRST loved us. It is our turn now.

Jennifer

Prayer Request

June 5

> "But thanks be to God, who always leads us as captives in Christ's triumphal procession and uses us to spread the aroma of Him everywhere."
>
> **2 CORINTHIANS 2:14**

The battle is already won! When we accepted Jesus into our hearts, He became our Hope, our Redeemer, and our Amazing Grace.

Put Him first place in your life. Watch the aroma of Him permeate every single area of your life when you truly love and adore Him. His sweet aroma will change the atmosphere in your home, your office, and everywhere that you go and in every situation you have in your life.

He loves you.

Jennifer

Prayer Request

June 6

"Do not be yoked together with unbelievers. For what do righteousness and wickedness have in common? Or what fellowship can light have with darkness?'

2 CORINTHIANS 6:14

This scripture is a hard one for me to digest! When I think about the compassion, acceptance, and unconditional love that Jesus showed to everyone, it seems counterintuitive to place a barrier between an unbeliever and a believer.

But here's the point: Yes, we are called to love everyone, but we are not called to "partner" or "yoke" ourselves with unbelievers. With whom are you yoked? Are you pulling in the same direction? This is not to encourage divorce but rather an opportunity to pray for your spouse or loved ones to join you in your dedication to the Lord.

When we align ourselves with someone in marriage, close friendships, or even business relationships, we need to be of one accord. You'll hear it referred to as a union, a meeting of the minds, a common core faith basis, whatever the popular term is called today, the fact still remains we are to follow scripture when making a decision about marrying an unbeliever or aligning yourself with unbelievers in significant business relationships or close friendships.

Jennifer

Prayer Request

June 7

> "Therefore encourage one another and build each other up, just as in fact you are doing."
>
> **1 THESSALONIANS 5:11**

How can you uplift someone today? Look around you and ask the Lord to reveal to you how you can help other people.

Frequently we may think that we will be able to help someone else if our finances improve or only if we would be able to make the "perfect" meal to deliver to a sick friend but here's the bottom line: JUST do it! Put some forward movement in your faith.

I truly believe that most people genuinely want to help others but allow passivity or perfectionism to stop them. Again, I encourage you to start today helping and encouraging others. Get busy helping others!

Jennifer

Prayer Request

June 8

> "I knew you before I formed you in your mother's womb. Before you were born I set you apart and appointed fit as my prophet to the nations."
>
> **JEREMIAH 1:5**

Do you know how special you are to God? Are you aware that you were created for a purpose? Does it make you glad to know that you were carefully designed and masterfully created by a loving God? You are totally awesome!

Friend, you are here on this planet for a reason. God has a plan for your life so why don't you get in agreement with Him and start living with His guidance? He is going to help you when you ask for His guidance and His blessing on your life.

Jennifer

Prayer Request

June 9

"I will be a Father to you, and you will be my sons and daughters, says the Lord Almighty."

2 CORINTHIANS 6:18

Did you grow up in a traditional family? Perhaps you were raised by a single parent or a grandparent? Or raised by a foster parent or an extended family member?

Families can bring us great strength but can also bring us deep sorrow. No one is perfect and families are no exception. Today you may be estranged from a family member. If so, I encourage you to pray for them and seek ways to repair the relationship, if possible.

Did you know that the Lord refers to you as His child? He refers to Himself as our Father! What a hope we have in Him and that hope is eternal.

Jennifer

Prayer Request

June 10

> "The faithful love of the Lord never ends! His mercies never cease. Great is His faithfulness; His mercies begin afresh every morning. I say to myself, 'The Lord is my inheritance; therefore, I will hope in Him!"
>
> **LAMENTATIONS 3:22-24**

Lamentations is a book in the Bible written by the "weeping prophet" named Jeremiah. Lamentations was written as a funeral song for the fallen city of Jerusalem. Despite the sadness of this particular book in the Bible, there is always a focus on where true HOPE can be found: The Lord.

Friend, I know that life can be overwhelming at times. I also know that there will be times when your heart will be heavy, perhaps mourning the loss of a loved one, a broken dream, or a failed friendship. But know this fact: Mercies are new each morning and God will give you the grace to move forward in every situation. He is WITH you!

I encourage you to keep your eyes fixed on Jesus. He is our source of strength and HOPE!

Jennifer

Prayer Request

June 11

> "Look at the birds. They don't plant or harvest or store food in barns, for your Heavenly Father feeds them. And aren't you far more valuable to Him than they are? Can all your worries add a single moment to your life?"
>
> **MATTHEW 6:26-27**

While sitting on my porch swing, I have the sweetest view of a pair of birds tending to a nest: one bird perched on the nest and the other bird repeatedly making food delivery trips back to the nest. It is a team effort to tend to that nest and they do it so well. And, hey, did I mention that they are just simple, sweet birds? The Lord takes care of them and the Lord will take care of you!

The Lord wants you to allow Him to care for you. Cast your burdens on Him, lean on Him, and learn to truly REST in His presence. He will sustain you. You and God make an unbeatable team!

Jennifer

Prayer Request

....

....

June 12

> "Seek the Kingdom of God above all else, and live righteously, and He will give you everything you need."
>
> **MATTHEW 6:33**

Who or what is on the THRONE of your life? If you're not sure, reflect on where you spend your time, your income, your energy, your passion, your focus: if God is not at the center of everything you do, who or what is the basis for your worship?

Do you idealize someone? Your spouse? Your child or grandchild? Is it a professional athlete? A famous actor? A friend? Is it yourself?

If it is not a person you worship, is it your career or a hobby? Is it a vehicle? Your home? Is it a relentless pursuit of perfectionism? Are you intentionally lazy to the point of being a sloth? Your life "plan" that must be executed perfectly? Is it holding on to past hurts, rehearsing them daily? Are you someone who portrays themselves as a martyr?

Friend, when we are instructed to SEEK God first and live righteously, it is the truth. SEEK Him and He will be found by you. Place HIM in first place in your life, above all else.

Jennifer

Prayer Request

June 13

"Don't be selfish; don't try to impress others. Be humble, thinking of others as better than yourselves. Don't look out only for your own interests, but take an interest in others, too."

PHILIPPIANS 2:3-4

If you've ever been around a selfish person, it can be emotionally draining. Constantly interrupting others to tell their stories, forcing others to follow their plans, having no interest in other people's lives, etc. are just a few selfish behaviors that can sabotage otherwise healthy relationships.

Are you genuinely interested in other people? Do you care about their feelings? Do you take an interest in your friends' hobbies, extracurricular activities, various likes/dislikes? I encourage you to examine yourself and your own behaviors.

Starting today let's all set the bar higher for unselfish actions! With the help of the Lord, we can place our focus on loving others like Jesus first loved us.

Jennifer

Prayer Request

June 14

> "So we are always confident, even though we know that as long as we live in these bodies we are not at home with the Lord. For we live by believing and not by seeing."
>
> **2 CORINTHIANS 5:6-7**

When Paul wrote this letter to the church at Corinth, he was sending instruction and encouragement to them. Those same words of encouragement are still applicable today!

How many times have you complained about your aches and pains today? I know I've certainly had some pains, to include an all day headache. But here's the fact: If we have those pesky aches and pains, it indicates that we are still alive and so we aren't finished with our assignment on earth yet.

As believers, we have hope and we have a secure future in eternity with our Lord. Ask the Lord to reveal to you the purpose and plan for your life and then do it! Believe Him to show you and He will do it!

Jennifer

Prayer Request

June 15

> "You say you have faith, for you believe there is one God. Good for you! Even the demons believe there this, and they tremble in terror. How foolish! Can't you see that faith without good deeds is useless?"
>
> **JAMES 2:19-20**

Put some actions behind your faith. If you see someone in need, don't simply say that you'll pray for them and walk in the other direction.

Yes, prayer is powerful. When you combine prayer with faith filled actions, it is even more powerful! Actions such as paying someone's bills, bringing a hot meal to a home bound person, donating business attire to someone searching for employment, visiting an elderly person at the nursing home, changing someone's flat tire, etc.. are examples of actions that show people you love them and care for their well-being.

Friend, the time is NOW to help others!

Jennifer

Prayer Request

June 16

"Don't you remember that our ancestor Abraham was shown to be right with God but his actions when he offered his son Isaac on the altar? You see, his faith and his actions worked together. His actions made his faith complete."

JAMES 3:21-22

What has God asked of you? Do you have a strong desire to start your own business, move to another city, go back to school, write a book, or develop a product? Is your heart's desire to start a family, adopt a child, sponsor someone to go on a mission trip? What exactly is it?

Pray about it. Ask God to give you wisdom and clarity regarding the situation. Ask God to keep your heart and mind open to what He wants to do in your life. Submit your requests to God.

And, my friend, if your request is in alignment with His will for your life, get ready! When He provides the vision, He makes the provision.

Jennifer

Prayer Request

June 17

"And so it happened just as the Scriptures say: Abraham believed God and God counted it as righteous because of his faith. He was even called a friend of God."

JAMES 2:23

Is God your number one priority? Seriously, is He your number one?

Placing God at the top of your priority list is the best way to live your life! We are uniquely designed to worship and adore our Heavenly Father.

He is your Creator and only He can fill the void that exists when someone doesn't know the Lord. What are you waiting for, friend? Reach out to Him and invite Him into your heart.

Jennifer

Prayer Request

....

....

June 18

> "For God bought you at a high price. So you must honor God with your body."
>
> **1 CORINTHIANS 6:20**

Our bodies are uniquely designed by God. We are special, valuable, and worthy of love.

Examine how you talk to yourself and how much time you spend comparing yourself to others. Get off the comparison "carousel" that spins around and around and arrives nowhere!

Every single part of you was designed by God. He loves you!

When you talk to yourself or about yourself, ensure that you are speaking life-filled words. You are a masterpiece!

Jennifer

Prayer Request

June 19

"So you have not received a spirit that makes you fearful slaves. Instead, you received God's Spirit when He adopted you as His own children. Now we call Him, 'Abba, Father. ' For His Spirit joins with our spirit to affirm that we are God's children."

ROMANS 8:15

As an adoptive parent, I can state that my adopted child has all the same legal rights as my biological child. I can also truthfully state that my adopted child is loved just as if he came from my womb: He. Is. My. Child.

This verse has great significance to those who are adopted or those whom have adopted a child. Adoption brings legal standing as a member of a family. I believe that when God says that we are His own children through His Spirit, He means it! What a family we have in the Lord!

Praise God!

Jennifer

Prayer Request

June 20

> "That is why we never give up. Though our bodies are dying, our spirits are being renewed every day."
>
> **2 CORINTHIANS 4:16**

This week I am attending a training conference at a resort. This particular resort was once quite prestigious but through the course of time, it has begun to show the effects of age. The various buildings on the property have a functional but well-used, weathered look about them. As humans, don't we have that same look as we become older?

Every single day we have an opportunity to go to the "Fountain of Youth" in our quiet time with the Lord. When we spend time in His presence, we are constantly being recharged and renewed in our spirit.

Spend time with the Lord! You'll be thankful that you did and you will not regret it.

Jennifer

Prayer Request

June 21

"We walk by faith, not by sight."

2 CORINTHIANS 5:7

Are you walking through something hard/tough/unpleasant, sweet friend? I know that sometimes life can present challenges and obstacles that we didn't see coming and believe me, I know! Sometimes we can be completely blindsided but yet our family and friends expect us to continue on as if nothing happened. It's hard. It's unpleasant. It's just not fair and it certainly isn't fun.

Yet this is what I know to be true: God is a good God and He is faithful. Stay the course and keep your eyes firmly focused on your Creator. He will sustain you today, tomorrow, and the rest of your life. If you don't feel close to God, who moved? He sure didn't!

When we see our future through eyes of faith, we are learning to walk in humble surrender to the Lord. Submit your life plans to Him and watch what HE WILL DO!

Jennifer

Prayer Request

June 22

"And we know that God causes everything to work together for the good of those who love God and are called to His purpose for them."

ROMANS 8:28

This world is chaotic. We currently are dealing with a worldwide health crisis, racial tensions, international conflict, financial challenges, and diverse political opinions. But know this, friend: God is still in control. I repeat, God is still in control!

Whatever is going on around us doesn't have to control our attitude. Allow God to take control of every area of your life, including your emotions! The roller coaster ride of emotional highs and lows can be circumvented but placing our TRUST in the Lord. He works ALL things together for our good as believers.

Read the scriptures and I encourage you to select some that apply directly to your particular situation. Memorize that particular scripture and apply it to your life. Repeat daily. Pray over that situation, injecting that particular scripture into your prayers. Watch how your emotions will start to level out as you place your TRUST in the Lord.

Jennifer

Prayer Request

June 23

"All things are possible with God."

MARK 10:27

Are you believing for a situation to turn around in your life? Your health, your finances, your career, your relationships? Are you becoming anxious about that situation because it is taking such a long time to be resolved?

Friend, I would be lying to you if I told you that I was always happy and constantly full of faith. I have times of sorrow, times of doubt, times of fear, times of regret, times of worry, and I realize that is because I am human. You are, too!

But hear me when I say this: I may be imperfect but God is PERFECT. I may be fickle but He is steadfast. I may worry and be filled with doubt but He is faithful. I may have regrets but He is full of Hope. I may become sad but He is true joy. If you haven't reached out to Him, do it now! Nothing is impossible for Him.

Jennifer

Prayer Request

....

....

June 24

> "If you need wisdom, ask our generous God, and He will give it to you. He will not rebuke you for asking."
>
> **JAMES 1:5**

There are times in life when you think you have all the answers. You're so confident that you know the answer before the question is asked. And you may also have times in life when you have absolutely no clue where to turn, what to say, how to behave, where to go, or what to do in a specific situation.

When you know that the ultimate source of wisdom is from the Lord, you realize that being plugged into that heavenly power source is right where you want to be every day and in every situation. Ask Him to guide you!

Jennifer

Prayer Request

June 25

"Don't let evil conquer evil you but conquer evil by doing good."

ROMANS 12:21

Has someone offended you lately? Has someone been unkind to one of your friends? Has an unfair situation seemed to take over your life? Has an ungrateful family member caused you to be discouraged?

Friend, listen to me: People are not perfect! Your feelings will get hurt, your mood will change like the wind, your closest friends may betray you, but know that God is always good. And He wants you to repay evil with GOOD!

Just do it.

Jennifer

Prayer Request

June 26

"Let all that you do be done in love."

1 CORINTHIANS 16:14

What the world needs now more than ever is LOVE! Think about what you're dwelling on in your mind. Are your thoughts of negativity or thoughts of positivity?

Friend, everything about the Lord is positive! He loves you unconditionally. He loves me unconditionally. Share your grateful heart with others today. Reach out to others with compassion, mercy, and grace.

Jennifer

Prayer Request

June 27

"If you confess with your mouth that Jesus is Lord and believe in your heart that God raised Him from the dead, you will be saved."

ROMANS 10:9

Do you know Jesus as your Lord and Savior? Do you believe that He died for YOU, that He rose from the dead, and that He is alive today? Sometimes it's easier to just assume that everyone already knows about Him and His incredible love for us but seriously, do you know Him?

None of us are perfect. No one. And contrary to popular belief, you don't have to be "cleaned up" before you surrender your life to Him.

Don't wait! He loves you exactly as you are–go ahead and accept His love and His grace!

Jennifer

Prayer Request

....

....

June 28

> "Don't you realize that your body is the temple of the Holy Spirit, who lives in you and was given to you by God? You do not belong to yourself, for God bought you with a high price. So you must honor God with your body."
>
> **1 CORINTHIANS 6:19-20**

You are so valuable to God! When He died on the cross for us, He sacrificed it all! Accept that marvelous gift!

Honor Him by taking care of your body, mind, and spirit. Watch your "appetite" for too much of the world. Learn to monitor what you watch on tv, listen to on your radio, discuss with others, and scroll through on your computer or phone.

We are not perfect. Mistakes will happen. Temptations occur. Confess it, accept His forgiveness, and move on to living the abundant life He wants you to have as a believer.

Jennifer

Prayer Request

June 29

> "Yet the Lord longs to be gracious to you; therefore He will rise up to show you compassion."
>
> **ISAIAH 30:18**

Are you a parent? When your child asks for something from you, most likely you attempt to purchase/borrow/locate that particular item for them, correct? And why do you do that for them? Because you love them and you want to do good for them.

Our Heavenly Father wants to be good to us as His children, too. He is always looking out for us. His resources are unlimited and His love and compassion for us is limitless. Seek His will in all you do and don't be afraid to ask Him for the desires of your heart. You are His child!

Jennifer

Prayer Request

....

....

June 30

"For the mountains may move and the hills disappear, but even then My faithful love for you will remain. My covenant of blessing will never be broken, 'says the Lord, who has mercy on you."

ISAIAH 54:10

Are you dealing with a mountain of debt, mountain of disappointment, mountain of regret, mountain of heartbreak? Whatever "mountain" you may be facing today, do you believe that God can move it? He can do it.

Trust Him. Believe in His power and steadfast love for you. He is merciful and He is a good, good Father.

Jennifer

Prayer Request

JULY

"I have told you these things, that My JOY and delight may be in you, and your JOY and gladness may be of full measure and complete and overflowing."

John 15:11

July 1

> "I have told you these things, that My JOY and delight may be in you, and your JOY and gladness may be of full measure and complete and overflowing."
>
> **JOHN 15:11**

When you believe and trust in the Lord, you can find rest. I agree that truly resting in the Lord is an ideal situation for all of us. Truly trusting in the Lord seems difficult in some situations but he is faithful and steadfast. His love for us is unconditional.

Start your day with prayer and end your day with prayer. When you spend time with Him, you become more joyful, peaceful, and merciful.

Jennifer

Prayer Request

....

....

July 2

"For God has not given us a spirit of fear
but of power, love, and a sound mind."

2 TIMOTHY 1:7

Are you making decisions in your life based on fear or based on faith? Fear will paralyze you but faith will mobilize you.

God has NOT given us a spirit of fear. Scripture repeatedly reinforces that God does not want us to live in a state of fear. The bible states this fact 365 times and I believe that it is a daily reminder for each of us that fear is not of God.

The Lord longs to be good to each one of us. He is a good, good Father. Trust Him with your life and remove fear from your decision making process.

Jennifer

Prayer Request

July 3

"So if the Son sets you free, you will be FREE indeed!"

JOHN 8:36

True freedom is knowing that you are unconditionally loved. When you accepted Jesus into your heart, He accepted you just as you are with unconditional love.

Reach out to Him in prayer. Thank Him for everything He has done for you and thank Him for your future. He has a wonderful plan for your life.

Jennifer

Prayer Request

July 4

"Work hard to enter the narrow gate to God's kingdom, for many will try to enter but will fail. When the master of the house has locked the door, it will be too late. You will stand outside knocking and pleading ' Lord, open the door for us! But He will reply, 'I don't know you or where you come from."

LUKE 13:24-25

Have you ever missed an opportunity and regretted it later? Perhaps it was a job opportunity, a romantic relationship, or a specific large purchase? Well, friend, if you regretted missing that opportunity, you'll deeply regret missing the opportunity to have everlasting life.

Have you accepted the Lord as your personal Savior? This is the time to do it and He is waiting for you!

Jennifer

Prayer Request

July 5

> "Once when He was eating with them, He commanded them, ' Do not leave Jerusalem until the Father sends you the gift He promised, as I told you before. John baptized with water but in just a few days you will be baptized with the Holy Spirit."
>
> **ACTS 1:4**

The Father, the Son, and the Holy Spirit comprise the Trinity. This is the divine mystery of Three in One!

My friend, know this: The Holy Spirit is a precious, sweet gift from the Lord. Go ahead and open your gift from the Lord!

The Holy Spirit is our comforter in times of sorrow, guides us in times of confusion, provides peace in times of chaos, convicts us in times of wrongdoing, strengthens us when we are weak, encourages us when we doubt, and the list goes on and on.

The Holy Spirit is our wonderful Helper.

Jennifer

Prayer Request

....

....

July 6

"I love the Lord because He hears my voice and my prayer for mercy. Because He bends down to listen, I will pray as long as I have breath!"

PSALM 116:1-2

This scripture verse shows just how tender our Lord is to us. It conjures up a picture of our Heavenly Father bending down, listening to our prayers, and truly hearing us.

There are times in life when it may seem like our prayers are not being heard but let me assure you of this: God still sits on the throne, He still cares for each one of us, He listens to our prayers, and He answers in His timing and His way. He is sovereign.

Peace to you and your families.

Jennifer

Prayer Request

July 7

"Be silent before the Lord, all humanity, for He is springing into action from His holy dwelling."

ZECHARIAH 2:13

We are in unprecedented times. It may seem as if God is being silent, allowing disease, political issues, racial division, and utter chaos to rule the Earth. Take heart, friend! HE IS STILL ON THE THRONE!

I truly believe that this is a time of God encouraging us to seek His heart, to know Him on a personal level, and to show each one of us that He is our sustainer and provider.

God is about to do something amazing!

Jennifer

Prayer Request

....

....

July 8

"Yes, a person is a fool to store up earthly wealth but not have a rich relationship with God."

LUKE 12:21

For the past several years I've been committed to eliminating debt in my life. And recently I finally become unencumbered by debt. Having said that, the new focus will be building up a savings account and retirement account.

Despite my best efforts, paying off debt wasn't a fast process and I predict that building extra savings will be a challenging task as well.

I'm not being trite when I say this but I know that savings accounts are a "tool" to assist me with having security for the future, but my main focus is and will remain being committed to what God wants to do in my life. He is the boss and He is whom I serve with my whole heart.

The LOVE of money is evil but money in and of itself is simply a useful tool to allow more choices in your life. Let your true LOVE be the Lord! That's a solid investment.

Jennifer

Prayer Request

July 9

"But not a single sparrow can fall to the ground without your Father knowing it. And the very hairs on your head are numbered. So don't be afraid; you are more valuable to God than a whole flock of sparrows."

MATTHEW 10: 29-30

Have you ever felt like God wasn't listening to your prayers? Ever felt like your prayer requests were pointless because nothing was happening? At times I admit that I can become discouraged when my prayers seem to be unanswered...even if the answer to my prayer request is a NO, I just want a clear and concise answer.

As a parent, I think about how much I love my children. Even if I don't agree with them on all of their requests of me, I love them and I am always interested in their academic and professional pursuits, their triumphs, their disappointments, their friendships, their activities, and their lives. Bottom line, my sweet children matter to me. I believe that being their mama is a privilege and an honor.

Don't you think our Heavenly Father cares for us more than we care for our own children? Friend, God Hears you, God Sees you, and God Loves you!

Jennifer

Prayer Request

July 10

"For the Lord will be your everlasting light. Your days of mourning will come to an end."

ISAIAH 60:20

How do you deal with sadness? I know that the typical response is to cry or to withdraw from others. Friend, let me encourage you to try a different approach next time you deal with sadness or depression: REACH out to others!

Here's an experiment for you: Take the focus off yourself and your own problems for just a day. Use that energy to write a letter, send a thank you card, deliver a small gift, clean up someone else's house for them, cook a meal for another person, purchase basic household necessities for a struggling newlywed couple, mow a neighbor's grass, or donate some of your NICE clothes to a charity.

Be helpful and encouraging to others. Watch how your own mood improves!

We are called to be the salt and light of this earth. Get busy spreading some joy to others. Don't wait to be blessed.... Go and BE THE BLESSING!

Jennifer

Prayer Request

July 11

> "Then the women of the town said to Naomi, 'Praise the Lord, Who has now provided a redeemer for your family! May this child be famous in Israel. May he restore your youth and care for you in your old age. For he is the son of your daughter-in-law who loves you and has been better to you than seven sons!"
>
> **RUTH 4:14-15**

When Naomi's husband died, she mourned. Then her two adult sons died. She became bitter, wanting to change her name to literally mean "bitter." But her daughter-in-law, Ruth, never left her side, even after Naomi encouraged her to return to her own homeland. They endured their situation (poverty, loss of marital status, homelessness) together.

Ruth showed true loyalty and it was ultimately rewarded. When Boaz, wealthy landowner, heard of her devotion to her mother-in-law, he specifically advised his workers to leave behind grain in the fields for her. He provided for her and eventually married her, having a child together that Naomi adored.

Boaz became her family line's kinsman redeemer to the point of being in the family lineage of Jesus! What an honor for Ruth and what a blessing for Naomi!

Who can you bless today? How can you leave behind some "grain" for someone on purpose? You are needed today to bless others! So start doing it today!

Jennifer

Prayer Request

....

....

July 12

"For God made Christ, who never sinned, to be the offering for our sin so that we could be made right with God through Christ."

2 CORINTHIANS 5:21

We are new creatures in Christ. Let Him renew you on a daily basis. Make your relationship with the Lord your number one priority.

I've noticed in my own life that when I truly submit my own will to His will for my life, there becomes a shift in my overall attitude towards those things that seemed insignificant or, in the alternative, those things that seemed insurmountable. He is with me and He is with you!

No problem is too small and no problem is too big for Him to handle. Pray and trust in His ability to transform situations for His glory.

Jennifer

Prayer Request

July 13

> "Let those who are wise understand these things.
> Let those with discernment listen carefully.
> The paths of the Lord are true and right, and
> righteous people live by walking in them. But
> in those paths sinners stumble and fall."
>
> **HOSEA 14:9**

Wisdom is crucial to living a life well lived. I repeat, Wisdom is crucial to living a life well-lived!

There is a difference between surviving and thriving. As believers, we have the assurance of eternity with Christ. But what about our life on earth? Should we be miserable here on earth as we wait for heaven? No, friend, no! It's fine to enjoy your life here!

We have been given the Holy Spirit to guide and advise us in all matters. Peace, love, joy, patience, wisdom, kindness, humility, self-control are some of the many gifts we have received.

Seek Wisdom in every area of your life. God placed unique talents, skills, and abilities within you. Develop them! Do not simply survive, make time to THRIVE in God's presence!

Jennifer

Prayer Request

July 14

"Then Christ will make His home in
your hearts as you trust Him."

EPHESIANS 3:17

I love this verse. The idea that Christ will "make His home" in my heart gives me such peace.

When we call someplace home, it describes a place of permanency, safety, and shelter. To think that the Creator of the Universe wants to dwell in my heart on a permanent basis is awe-inspiring!

I encourage you today to invite Christ into your life. Trust Him with your future. He's got you!

Jennifer

Prayer Request

July 15

"Always work enthusiastically for the Lord, for you know that nothing you do for the Lord is ever useless."

1 CORINTHIANS 15:58

Ever have one of those days or weeks or months or years when you feel like your hard work is unappreciated, underpaid, undervalued, disrespected, or insignificant? Are you sick and tired of being sick and tired at the office? Please know that it happens to all of us! We are HUMAN!

I recommend capturing this scripture on your computer, your car dashboard, your bathroom mirror, anywhere you look on a regular basis. When you shift your focus to believe that you are working for the Lord, a shift happens! You begin to glorify Him in everything you do with a great attitude and a spirit of EXCELLENCE!

Jennifer

Prayer Request

....

....

July 16

"Imitate God, therefore, in everything you do, because you are His dear children."

EPHESIANS 5:1

Imitate God in everything you do! That's a tall order, isn't it? He's perfect and we are human.

When we accepted Him into our hearts, He began to dwell in us. Allow the Holy Spirit to edify, encourage, and counsel you. Every day our goal should be to be more like Christ in our thoughts, words, and deeds. The goal is to pursue Him with everything we do!

Jennifer

Prayer Request

July 17

> "So stop telling lies. Let us tell our neighbors the truth, for we are all parts of the same body."
>
> **EPHESIANS 4:25**

Stop telling lies. Just stop it. Easier said than actually done, correct? Lies don't have to be huge whoppers. Lies can little deceptions. Lies can even be the things we tell ourselves. Don't be fooled by lies! God came for us to have an abundant life and joy overflowing!

The enemy came to steal, kill, and destroy. One of the ways that the enemy gets a stronghold is by "wrong thinking" in what we tell ourselves.

Friend, don't listen to the enemy. Listen to what God says about you: you are a masterpiece! You are forgiven, redeemed, accepted, chosen, loved, set apart, and righteous. Believe the TRUTH and rebuke the lie.

Jennifer

Prayer Request

....

....

July 18

"All of this is for your benefit. And as God's grace reaches more and more people, there will be great thanksgiving, and God will receive more and more glory."

2 CORINTHIANS 4:15

God works everything out for good for those who love Him and who are called according to His purpose. Knowing that fact brings me great comfort as I encounter obstacles and deal with issues in my own life. What about you? Whom do you trust with your fears of the future?

Friend, we have not been promised a trouble-free life but we have been promised that our Lord will never leave us nor forsake us. What are you dealing with today? I encourage you to reach out to Him in prayer and in faith, trusting that He will give you exactly what you need when you need it.

Jennifer

Prayer Request

July 19

"When someone has been given much, much will be required in return and when someone has been entrusted with much even more will be required."

LUKE 12:48

How has God blessed you? With good health? Large and loving family? Wonderful support system of friends? Terrific career? Smoothly running household? Financial freedom? Fabulous personality? Creativity and Vision?

I encourage you right now to take an inventory of whatever God has blessed you with in this life. Those gifts need to be surrendered back to Him to bring about His will on earth. How exactly does this process of surrender happen?

For example, you may question whether you are supposed to give away all of your finances and become destitute? No, certainly not....ask the Lord how He wants you to direct your finances to bless and encourage others. What talents and abilities has He given you? Develop those talents and bless others with it. What areas of gifts seem to occur easily and naturally with you? Pay attention to your own gifts within you. Those natural gifts are there to bless others!

Don't hide your gifts under a basket. Develop them, Show them, Use them to glorify our Creator!

Jennifer

Prayer Request

. . . .

. . . .

July 20

"Who can find s virtuous and capable wife? She is more precious than rubies. Her husband can trust her, and she will greatly enrich his life."

PROVERBS 31:10-11

When someone can truly trust you, that is such a compliment to you. They will lean on you, come to you for advice, bring you into their confidence. Being a trustworthy person is an admirable goal for all of us. As believers in the Lord, we have the best role model: Jesus Christ. In Him we have complete trust and comfort.

When there is trust between individuals, there is safety. When someone feels safe and secure, they will blossom and develop to their full potential. Friend, I encourage you today to become a TRUSTWORTHY person in every relationship you have and watch how it will enrich your life and the lives of others!

Jennifer

Prayer Request

July 21

> "She brings him good, not harm, all the days of her life. She finds wool and flax and busily spins it. She is like a merchant's ship, bringing her food from afar. She gets up before dawn to prepare breakfast for her household and plan the day's work for her servant girls."
>
> **PROVERBS 31:13-15**

Working towards a common goal makes a team! In your own family, do you have "team" goals? Do you have shared interests, passions, dreams, and long-term goals within your family? If not, I encourage you to begin having those conversations with your family!

Focus on the good in your family and begin to bless each member of your "team" as you move towards common goals. Pray for one another, communicate clearly, and take care of each other. Your family is your gift from God.

Jennifer

Prayer Request

. . . .

. . . .

July 22

"The temptations in your life are no different from what others experience. And God is faithful. He will not allow the temptation to be more than you can stand. When you are tempted, He will show you a way out so that you can endure."

1 CORINTHIANS 10: 13

Will we be tempted in our lives? Yes. And each one of us may be tempted in areas that are unique to us. For instance, one person may be tempted by smoking, another person by alcohol, and another by overeating. Some people overspend and some people are prone to being dishonest, others may find themselves wanting to gossip about others. Each one of us will have our own set of temptations!

When temptation occurs, what are we to do as Christians? Take God at His word.

He said He would provide a way out so that we could endure and He will do it. Ask Him to lead you down the BEST path for your life, follow His teachings, and avoid situations where you know you will be tempted in your areas of weakness.

TRUST Him.

Jennifer

Prayer Request

July 23

"Her hands are busy spinning thread, her fingers twisting fiber. She extends a helping hand to the poor and opens her arms to the needy. She has no fear of winter for her household, for everyone has warm clothes."

PROVERBS 31:19-21

Planning for the future is wise. While it is important to live in the moment and enjoy each day, there needs to be a balance in planning, saving, and investing in your future.

If you haven't planned or saved for your future, do not despair! Ask God for wisdom and discipline. Follow His leading to making wise choices in your spending habits, debt repayment, and work ethic. He will guide you but you need to be open to His instruction.

Jennifer

Prayer Request

July 24

"She makes her own bedspreads. She dresses in fine linen and purple gowns. Her husband is well known at the city gates, where he sits with the other civic leaders. She makes belted linen garments and sashes to sell to the merchants."

PROVERBS 31: 22-24

Money is not evil. I repeat, money is not evil! The ***love*** of money is described as evil.

Money, in and of itself, is simply a tool. It's a tool that allows us to have choices.

There is a balance of obtaining choices for your present situation (day to day living expenses), your future situation (savings and investments) and your past situation (debts). Debt is like a huge weight chained to you, dragging you down and following you everywhere. As Christians, we are to "owe" our brother nothing except love.

I encourage you to review your family financial plan, to include debt repayment and savings. This is not meant to discourage you but rather encourage you! There are lots of Christian based financial plans available. Conduct some research and see which plan works best for your family.

Jennifer

Prayer Request

July 25

"Three things will last forever-faith, hope, and love-and the greatest of these is love."

1 CORINTHIANS 13

You can be a person of great faith who believes that mountains can be moved. You can be a person who has tremendous hope in Christ and all His promises. But love conquers all.

He first loved us. And because He loved us so much, He gave up His only Son. Love is powerful. Love lasts forever.

Whom has the Lord placed in your life to love? Who makes you laugh? Who makes fun of you and hurts your feelings? Who tells you the truth? Who lies to you or about you? Who causes you grief? Who causes you joy? Who brings you gifts? Who steals from you? Who blesses you? Who curses you? Love them anyway!

It's all about Christ's LOVE.

Jennifer

Prayer Request

July 26

"Obey your spiritual leaders, and do what they say. Their work is to watch over your souls, and they are accountable to God. Give them reason to do this with joy and not with sorrow. That would certainly not be for your benefit."

HEBREWS 13:17

Who is your spiritual leader? Your pastor, priest, youth group leader, worship team leader? You may have several leaders or you may have none that come to mind.

It is wonderful if you are blessed to be surrounded by faithful, dedicated, committed Christian leaders. If you are not, I encourage you to research local churches in your area, go online to connect with church services, listen to encouraging podcasts, read uplifting books, and find a mentor!

Put forth a little bit of effort in seeking the Lord. Make Him your first priority and watch Him transform every area of your life.

Jennifer

Prayer Request

July 27

> "This means that anyone who belongs to Christ has become a new person. The old life is gone; a new life has begun!"
>
> **2 CORINTHIANS 5:17**

Are you feeling ashamed today because of past mistakes or wrong decisions? Do you have remorse over making major decisions without praying about it first? Have you hastily entered into a relationship and now you have deep regrets? Friend, we are all human and we all make mistakes.

Here's the key: take your regrets, concerns, failures, sorrow, anxiety, despair, whatever is causing you stress and leave it on the altar with God. He has broad shoulders and He can carry the load. Let Him love you as His precious child. He will guide you on the best path for your life. He's a good good Father!

Jennifer

Prayer Request

....

....

July 28

> "That is why we never give up. Though our bodies are dying, our spirits are being renewed every day."
>
> **2 CORINTHIANS 4:16**

Do you exercise on a regular basis? If so, that is good!

Do you eat well and obtain restful sleep every day? Wonderful!

Do you have a household budget that you adhere to in order to protect your family's financial future? Terrific!

How about spending time with the Lord on a daily basis? If so, that is great! If not, let me encourage you.

Yes, we are instructed to take care of our bodies and our finances but we would be unwise if we ignore spending time with our Creator. When I say unwise, I specifically mean that spending time with the Lord on a regular basis is the best "investment" that we will ever make in our lives.

Jennifer

Prayer Request

July 29

> "And may you have the power to understand, as all God's people should, how wide, how long, how high, and how deep His love is."
>
> **EPHESIANS 3:18**

God loves you.

I repeat, God loves you.

And again, God loves you.

No matter what you've done, no matter who you are, no matter where you are, know this: You are His child and He loves you.

Receive His love today. It is simple but so profound to acknowledge that He is sovereign and He loves each one of us.

Jennifer

Prayer Request

....

....

July 30

"Ask, using My name, and you will receive, and you will have abundant joy."

JOHN 16:24

I sure do love this verse! What a comfort to know that God wants to be involved in a relationship with us. He's interested in the little daily needs and the big requests, the inconsequential and the important, all of it!

I'm not saying that the Lord is Santa Claus in gift giving but hear me on this: I truly believe that God loves each one of us, created us for a unique purpose, instilled gifts & talents within us, and He delights in our success. If you need something, . Yes, I said that because our Lord is a good, good Father.

When we ask for the Lord to bless us and He does so, we have a responsibility to bless others. He doesn't give us gifts of money, food surplus, clothing, houses, cars, merely to hoard or stockpile them. I encourage you to become creative in blessing others with your blessings!

Jennifer

Prayer Request

July 31

> "He will cover you with His feathers. He will shelter you with His wings. His faithful promises are your armor and protection."
>
> **PSALM 91:4**

Friend, are world events causing you to be scared or afraid of the future? Are you barely holding on? Does this world seem like it is in total and complete chaos?

DO NOT FEAR. God's got this and God's got YOU!

Seek Him and His will. Do you have big prayer requests? It's okay, no worries: God has big shoulders and He can be trusted. He's faithful, loyal, and completely in love with you! Let Him shelter and protect you.

Jennifer

Prayer Request

....

....

AUGUST

"This is My Son, whom I love; with whom I am well pleased."

Matthew 3:17

August 1

> "This is My Son, whom I love; with whom I am well pleased."
>
> **MATTHEW 3:17**

What a complete confirmation of God's love for Jesus!

Isn't it a wonderful when someone publicly confirms that they approve of you and love you? Look around you and ask yourself whom you could bless today with your words. Bless someone with your words in public. Let the world know that you respect them and honor them.

Acknowledgement that someone has done something wonderful is a way to show them respect and allows them to be blessed in the presence of others.

Bless, bless, bless others!

Jennifer

Prayer Request

....

....

August 2

"For where two or three gather in My name, there am I with them."

MATTHEW 18:20

There is power in agreement. Do you have friends who pray with you and pray for you? Do you pray for others?

It is wonderful to see prayers being answered. It is especially wonderful when you have prayed with others about a specific need that someone has and then see that prayer request being answered. The entire group celebrates together!

I encourage you to continue to pray with others and for others. If you don't have someone to pray with you, ask God for wisdom to locate a praying friend. A friend who prays with you and for you is a true friend indeed. God bless you, friend!

Jennifer

Prayer Request

August 3

"My child, listen when your father corrects you. Don't neglect your mother's instruction. What you learn from them will crown you with grace and be a chain of honor around your neck."

PROVERBS 1:8-9

Honor your parents! Show them respect, even when you disagree with them. Show them honor, even if they've done dishonorable actions. Show them love and take care of them when they need it. They are your parents and it is biblical to honor them.

Parents aren't perfect! Parenting is a job in which few of us have ever had any formal training. It's a job in which everything is learned through "on the job" training or experience. It's a tough job.

Either through movies, television series, friends, books we read, we repeatedly hear stories about how someone's parents messed up their lives. It's like a blame-game where everyone points their fingers at either a lack of parenting (absentee parent) or, in the alternative, someone being a helicopter parent (hovering over their child).

Let me ask you, did your parents make some mistakes in raising you? Parents are humans, too. Show your parents some grace and extend mercy when needed. And most importantly, love them.

Jennifer

Prayer Request

....

....

August 4

> "For the Lord grants wisdom! From His mouth come knowledge and understanding. He grants a treasure of common sense to the honest. He is a shield to those who walk with integrity. He guards the path of the just and protects those who are faithful to Him."
>
> **PROVERBS 2:6-8**

Wisdom is precious! Seek the Lord and follow His direction and leading of the Holy Spirit in your life. How do you do that? Through prayer and reading the Bible. His word never fails!

When we have wisdom, we make the best decisions in every area of our lives. I encourage you to seek and actively pursue wisdom more than you ever have in your life. The world and current events are ever-evolving but the Lord is the same yesterday, today, and tomorrow. His love and His wisdom never fail!

Jennifer

Prayer Request

August 5

> "Truly I tell you whatever you bind on earth will be bound in heaven, and whatever you loose on earth will be loosed in heaven."
>
> **MATTHEW 18:18**

What concerns you today? What ideas, hopes, dreams do you have buried in your heart? What fears, insecurities, and doubts do you harbor?

I encourage you to release your hurts to the Lord and forgive those who wronged you. I've heard it said that holding on to bitterness is like drinking poison and expecting someone else to die. It sounds ridiculous but that is exactly what bitterness is... an absurd waste of time, effort, and energy.

This may seem impossible but it is not impossible when you invite God in His sovereignty and mercy to assist you. Just ask the Lord to help heal your heart and your hurts.

Jennifer

Prayer Request

....

....

August 6

"Two people are better than one, for they can help each other succeed. If one person falls, the other can reach out and help. But someone who falls alone is in real trouble."

ECCLESIASTES 4:9-10

Partnerships can be very beneficial. An alliance with another person can bring a fresh strength to difficult situations. And when two people are in agreement, they form a powerful force against anything that comes against them.

With whom are you in agreement with regarding your life? Are you surrounding yourself with people who speak life over you, your dreams, your family, your future, your career, your finances? If not, please start TODAY! Pray for God to bring the right people in your life at the right time and in the right way.

Jennifer

Prayer Request

August 7

"For we are not making up clever stories when we told you about the powerful coming of our Lord Jesus Christ. We saw His majestic splendor with our own eyes when He received honor and glory from God the Father. The voice from the majestic glory of God said to Him, ' This is my dearly loved Son, who brings me great joy.' We ourselves heard that voice from heaven when we were with Him on the holy mountain."

2 PETER 1:16-18

Peter was an eyewitness to this incredible event of God identifying Jesus as His Son in the presence of others. An eyewitness has the knowledge to identify a person, place, or event because they actually saw it.

Additionally, Peter, along with the other apostles. saw the people and impossible situations where Jesus performed miracles.

As a former prosecutor, I understand the importance and impact that a credible witness can have on proving the facts in a case. Here, Peter, accompanied by James and John, was one of the eyewitnesses who saw Jesus being transfigured with white clothing and radiant light. God spoke and three apostles heard Him state that Jesus was His beloved Son.

Friend, if you haven't accepted Jesus into your heart, what are you waiting for to make that decision? Reach out to the Lord.

Jennifer

Prayer Request

August 8

"Be anxious for nothing, but in everything by prayer and supplication with thanksgiving let your requests be made known to God."

PHILIPPIANS 4:6

Are you feeling anxious? Does the world around you appear to be out of control?

Have you prayed about whatever is troubling you? If the answer hasn't arrived, keep praising, keep praying, keep standing in faith, and keep your head held high. God loves you and He sees you!

You are a child of God, uniquely designed for a purpose. Pray that God will infuse you with passion and purpose to bring Him glory. Your best days are ahead of you!

Jennifer

Prayer Request

August 9

"A wise child brings joy to a father; a foolish child brings grief to a mother."

PROVERBS 10:1

Were your parents "perfect" parents to you? If so, good for you! If not, please remember that they still need to be respected. When we respect our parents, we are planting good seeds into the ground for a harvest of generational blessings.

We should always strive to be respectful to our parents, no matter our age or level of maturity. When we show honor and respect to our parents, it sows a good seed that will grow into a bountiful harvest of blessings for generations.

Respect, Honor, and Blessings.

Jennifer

Prayer Request

August 10

"I am the Lord and I do not change."

MALACHI 3:6

I live in the same town where I grew up as a child. To some people, that may seem stifling. For me, it is a great source of comfort to be surrounded by family, childhood friends, and lots of familiarity. I love to drive around my town and look at old buildings, favorite businesses, historic landmarks, and point them out to whomever is riding with me. I like that while the entire world may seem in constant chaos, my hometown remains the same in many aspects.

How comforting to know that our Lord NEVER changes. What He says, He means! What He says about you never changes: You are His child. You are the apple of His eye. You are created for a purpose. You are a friend of God.

Get this firmly rooted in your mind: God isn't fickle. God is rock steady and HE LOVES YOU!

Jennifer

Prayer Request

August 11

> "Truly, I tell you," Jesus answered," today-yes, tonight, before the rooster crows twice, you yourself will disown me three times."
>
> **MARK 14:30**

When Jesus told Peter that he would disown Him, Peter was adamant that he would never do that but He surely did! Remember, this is the same hot tempered man who cut off the ear of a guard who came to arrest Jesus. Peter loved Jesus but Peter was also an imperfect man. Just like each one of us.

And that same imperfect man is the ROCK upon whom the church was built! Friend, whatever you've done and wherever you are in life, know this: GOD LOVES YOU and has a plan for your life. Submit your whole heart to Him, repent, and surrender your life to the Lord. He is worthy of your affection and adoration.

Trust Him to use your imperfections as a testimony of His goodness and grace.

Jennifer

Prayer Request

....

....

August 12

> "Love the Lord your God with all your heart and with all your soul and with all your strength and with all your mind' and, 'Love your neighbor as yourself."
>
> **LUKE 10:21**

All your HEART: Ask Jesus into your heart.

All your SOUL: Share the Gospel.

All your STRENGTH: Your energy focused on pursuing what God's will is for your life.

All your MIND: Dwell on His promises.

Love your neighbor as yourself. Start sharing, start caring, and start loving the people around you!

Jennifer

Prayer Request

August 13

> "I am the Vine; you are the branches. If you remain in Me and I in you, you will bear much fruit; apart from Me you can do nothing."
>
> **JOHN 15:5**

I'm from the South and we have lots of sayings that sound ridiculous, I know! We make statements such as "fixin" to do something, having "roots" in our hometown, all sodas are called "coke", and so forth.

Well, where are your "roots?" Mine are deeply planted in my hometown, where I was raised, attended school and church, and where I remain here today with my children. And my roots are also planted in Jesus Christ and His unfailing love for me. What about you, friend?

No matter what is happening in our world today, I know that my eternal future is secure and that brings me such great JOY! I encourage you to get connected to the TRUE Vine and allow Him to transform your life.

Jennifer

Prayer Request

....

....

August 14

"This is My command: Love each other."

JOHN 15:17

It is not complicated. It really isn't.

LOVE the Lord with your whole heart.

LOVE EACH OTHER. And love isn't always easy. It is an action verb. Decide today that you will love those people whom the Lord places in your life.

What if the annoy you? Love them anyway.

What if they offend you? Love them anyway.

What if they pester you? Love them anyway.

What if they disrespect you? Love them anyway.

What if they discredit you? Love them anyway.

Friend, those are your people and your assignment. Love them well.

Jennifer

Prayer Request

August 15

> "But they could not stand up against the wisdom the Spirit gave him as he spoke."
>
> **ACTS 6:10**

Stephen was a man described as "full of God's grace and power" and when he spoke to the crowds, wonders and signs occurred. Naturally, this attracted the attention of some "haters", but they could not stop him from continuing to do the Lord's work. Are haters stopping you from doing the work that God has called you to do?

Stephen eventually was stoned to death because of his unwavering faith and courage in sharing the Gospel. At one point his face is actually described as the face of an Angel while he was being questioned for his beliefs. That is a powerful testimony to his unwavering faith.

Friend, I encourage you to read your Bible. It is full of life and wisdom.

Jennifer

Prayer Request

August 16

"Those who cling to worthless idols turn away from God's love for them. But I, with shouts of grateful praise will sacrifice to You. What I have vowed I will make good. I will say, 'Salvation comes from the Lord.'"

JONAH 2:8-9

Jonah uttered these words while he was literally in the belly of a whale. It sounds incredible, doesn't it? To sing praises inside of a smelly old whale?

God had previously commanded him to go to Nineveh to preach against the wickedness in it but Jonah decided to flee to Tarshish via a ship. Jonah thought he could hide from God in the ship as it sailed in the sea.

Maybe this biblical tale seems unreal but here's what I know: after Jonah straightened up his attitude, started praising God, the whale vomited him on dry land to finally begin his trek to Nineveh. And in Nineveh he did exactly as the Lord instructed him to preach to the citizens of Nineveh for repentance.

Friend, what are you running from today? I encourage you to quit running from God and run towards Him.

Jennifer

Prayer Request

August 17

"The Lord gives His people strength. The Lord blesses them with peace."

PSALM 29:11

Peace. For some people, peace is a word that is associated with holding up 2 fingers in a salute for an Instagram photo. For other people, peace signifies the absence of turmoil in their lives. For others, peace is another word to express harmony and unity.

God's peace is very unique because it passes all human understanding. When we submit ourselves to His will for our lives, His peace will begin to fortify and strengthen us for every challenge.

Friend, I encourage you to protect your peace. And true peace comes from the Lord. Submit to Him and allow Him to work in your life.

Jennifer

Prayer Request

August 18

"Honor the Lord for the glory of His name, Worship the Lord in the splendor of His holiness."

PSALM 29:2

HONOR is such a powerful word. To show honor is to show respect. Whom are you honoring in your life? Your parents, your employer, your friends, and/or your family members?

To show honor is a sign of strength. To show honor is a sign of humility. To show honor is a sign of gratitude.

Honor the Lord. He is absolutely worth it!

Jennifer

Prayer Request

August 19

> "I entrust my spirit into Your hand. Rescue me, Lord, for You are a faithful God."
>
> **PSALM 31:5**

Prayer for today: Lord, please rescue us in situations in which we are desperately needing your strength to survive through the process of developing character, wisdom, and endurance.

Guide us, direct us, and protect us as we bring our plans and hopes in alignment with Your will for our lives. Your strength is sufficient for us and you are faithful to complete the good work you started in each of us.

Thank you for always being such a faithful God.

Jennifer

Prayer Request

....

....

August 20

> "You have turned my mourning into joyful dancing. You have taken away my clothes of mourning and clothed me with joy, that I might sing praises to You and not be silent. O Lord, my God, I will give You thanks forever!"
>
> **PSALM 30:11-12**

Thank God Almighty!

Today is the day to praise Him in advance of starting your workday, your school day, your weekend, receiving your health report, reviewing your bank account statement, making your plans, establishing your thoughts, maintaining your attitude, and the "everything else" in your day. Thank Him and PRAISE Him!

He is a mighty deliverer and He is worthy of praise. Come on, friend, get your praise on!

Jennifer

Prayer Request

August 21

> "I will exalt you, Lord, for You rescued me. You refused to let my enemies triumph over me."
>
> **PSALM 30:1**

The best defender you'll ever have is Jesus Christ. The best advocate you'll ever have is Jesus Christ. The best friend you'll ever have is Jesus Christ.

He will not fail you and He is FAITHFUL to finish what He started in you. Seek Him and His will for your life.

When you place Him as your first priority in your life, you will see Him work miracles and move mountains in your life. He is worthy to be praised and He will triumph over your enemies for you!

Jennifer

Prayer Request

....

....

August 22

"Work with enthusiasm, as though you were working for the Lord rather than for people. Remember that the Lord will reward each one of us for the good we do, whether we are slaves or free."

EPHESIANS 6:7-8

Are you burned out at work? Stressed out at work? Dreading walking into the office? Friend, if this describes you, know that you are not alone! Even the best jobs have their own set of issues.

When Paul wrote this encouraging word to the faithful church at Ephesus, he knew the daily struggles that they did and would encounter on a daily basis in their employment. It is such a comfort to know that those words written so many years ago can encourage us even today?

Are you still stressed, frustrated, disappointed at work? Here's the remedy: REMEMBER whom you truly work for: The Lord! It's a game changer!

Jennifer

Prayer Request

August 23

"He grants a treasure of common sense to the honest, He is a shield to those who walk with integrity. He guards the path of the just and protects those who are faithful to Him."

PROVERBS 2:7-8

Do you need wisdom? Do you need protection? Re-read that scripture passage from Proverbs. The Lord will grant wisdom to you and a healthy dose of common sense.

You need to ASK Him for wisdom and then follow His leading and go where He guides you. It may be to study a certain subject, locate a mentor, or develop a new skill.

There are other times the Lord may be leading you to slow your pace, be still, listen to Him, and then move in the direction He leads. Whatever the situation and whatever the need, know that HE IS WITH YOU ALWAYS and He is your shield of protection.

Jennifer

Prayer Request

August 24

> "My child, listen when your father corrects you. Don't neglect your mother's instruction. What you learn from them will crown you with grace and be a chain of honor around your neck."
>
> **PROVERBS 1:8-9**

Honoring our parents is biblical. When we honor and respect our parents, it shows deference to authority and wisdom. Having said that, does that mean that our parents are infallible? Certainly not! Parents, take the pressure off yourselves and know that only the Lord is perfect.

How is your relationship with your parents? Do you love them? Do you respect them and their authority over you? Sometimes it takes several years for parents and children to have a wonderful relationship.

I currently have one teenager left in the home and I will admit that it has been a daily struggle trying to engage that particular child in completing schoolwork, attending church, forming hygiene habits, and consistently using good manners. And trust me, the struggle is REAL! But I refuse to give up and give in to take an easier path of parenthood because good parenting is tough parenting.

And I know that I know that I KNOW that prayer works! So parents, keep parenting! And your children will honor you and call blessed.

Jennifer

Prayer Request

August 25

> "Trust in the Lord with ALL your heart; do not depend on your own understanding. Seek His will in all you do, and He will show you which path to take."
>
> **PROVERBS 3:5-6**

Do you find it difficult to trust others? What about your friendships? Romantic relationships? Is there a history/pattern of broken trust? Has your heart been broken, your life shattered, your dreams unfulfilled because of the actions of another person?

Friend, let Jesus restore your trust! He is faithful, unshakable, unwavering, devoted, committed, and solid as a rock. Build your life upon trusting Him, day by day, and watch your heart be restored and your life renewed. TRUST in Him with your whole heart. He is praiseworthy!

Jennifer

Prayer Request

....

....

August 26

"As the beating of cream yields butter
and striking the nose causes bleeding, so
stirring up anger causes quarrels."

PROVERBS 30:33

Do you watch television shows that involve family situations? Many of the shows seem to only show discord and strife between family members, almost as if to promote a sense of total chaos within the family. While we may laugh at their theatrics, it may seem all too real when we ponder our own family situations.

Do you have a family member whom everyone ridicules, even if seemingly in jest? Are there times when you exclude a family member from events because you think they may embarrass you? Are there long-standing quarrels between family members that need to be resolved?

Friend, life on this earth is short! Forgive your family members. Love them, care for them, and PRAY for them! Your family is NOT the enemy's playground so don't allow strife to set in between your precious loved ones.

Jennifer

Prayer Request

August 27

> "Someone may say to you, 'Let's ask the mediums and those who consult the spirits of the dead. With their whispering sand muttering, they will tell us what to do.' But shouldn't people ask God for guidance? Should the living seek guidance from the dead?"
>
> **ISAIAH 8:19**

Have you ever consulted with a palm reader, fortune teller, or used a horoscope to "predict" your future? According to scripture, we should ask the living God for guidance in our lives.

While it may seem harmless and fun to read a horoscope, know this: God is the Ultimate authority on our lives. Not a horoscope, not a fortune teller, not a tea leaf, not a fortune cookie! God is God and He is very much alive!

Our Lord is omniscient, ever-present, and He is sovereign. His ways are not our ways. So the next tine you are seeking guidance in any area of your life, go to the ultimate source of wisdom: GOD!

Jennifer

Prayer Request

....

....

August 28

"Keep on asking, and you will receive what you ask for. Keep on seeking, and you will find. Keep on knocking, and the door will be opened to you. For everyone who asks, receives. For everyone who seeks, finds. And to everyone who knocks, the door will be opened."

MATTHEW 7:7-8

At one time in my life, this was my all-time favorite scripture. Literally, I recited it so much it became my private mantra. Having said that, the application of this scripture doesn't mean that God becomes a super-sized Santa Claus: such as, say the prayer and whatever we want falls immediately into our lap!

When we accepted Jesus Christ into our heart as our Savior, we have everlasting life with Him. That fact alone is enough to celebrate!

But Jesus doesn't leave us on this earth without His supernatural resources. His PEACE, His JOY, His STRENGTH, His WISDOM, His LOVE, His HUMILITY, His SELF-CONTROL, His HEALING, His PROVISION, His RESURRECTION POWER, His KINDNESS, and His GRACE. Unlimited resources.

Keep Asking. Keep Seeking, Keep Knocking. He is Our amazing Lord.

Jennifer

Prayer Request

August 29

> "For God is working in you, giving you the desire and the power to do what pleases Him."
>
> **PHILIPPIANS 2:13**

Are you a people pleaser? Are you constantly trying to make other people happy? Or are you someone who runs from one activity to another with a "to-do" list, checking off the items of completion? Perhaps you're sedentary, lying on the couch most of your days, waiting for others to serve you?

When we accepted Jesus as our Savior, He gave us eternal life. By trusting in Him and allowing Him through the Holy Spirit to mold us and shape us, we grow and develop into exactly whom He designed us to be for His glory.

Jennifer

Prayer Request

August 30

> "Therefore, since we are surrounded by such a huge crowd of witnesses to the life of faith, let us strip off every weight that slows us down, especially the sin that so easily trips us up. And let us run with endurance the race God has set before us. We do this by keeping our eyes on Jesus, the champion who initiates and perfects our faith."
>
> **HEBREWS 12:1-2**

What is hindering you today? Are you weighed down with guilt? Remorse? Memories? Past failures? Betrayal? Fear of rejection?

Friend, THROW whatever is holding you back and run your race! Jesus loves you. You are forgiven. You are set free. Quit looking back and press forward as you develop your trust in the Lord to guide and direct your steps. Let Jesus be your champion, directing and guiding you.

Jennifer

Prayer Request

August 31

"Then Christ will make His home in your hearts as you trust in Him. Your roots will grow down into God's love and keep you strong."

EPHESIANS 3:17-18

Who or what lives in your heart? If you don't know the answer, think about what you think about: WHAT or WHOM are you thinking about on a continual basis? What you replay in your mind becomes your reality.

When you accept Jesus as your Savior, let Him also become your Lord. The Lord of your life. The Lord of your home. The Lord of your family. The Lord of your relationships. The Lord of your finances. The Lord of your career. The Lord of your body. The Lord of your everyday. The Lord of your future. The Lord of your thoughts.

The Lord who loves you.

Jennifer

Prayer Request

....

....

SEPTEMBER

"Trust in the Lord with all your heart; do not depend on your own understanding. Seek His will in all you do, and He will show you which path to take."

Proverbs 3:5-6

September 1

> "Trust in the Lord with all your heart; do not depend on your own understanding. Seek His will in all you do, and He will show you which path to take."
>
> **PROVERBS 3:5-6**

Do you make wise or rash decisions on a regular basis? Are your decisions indicative of your beliefs? Do you ever regret decisions made due to impulse spending or immaturity?

Friend, we are all imperfect humans! And as humans, our frailty becomes readily apparent when we view our lives from a rear view mirror. Mistakes are made as a part of life. Learn from your mistakes and move forward with your life.

NOW is the time to use God-given wisdom in every area of your life! Pray about it, seek wise counsel, and follow the leading of the Holy Spirit.

Jennifer

Prayer Request

....

....

September 2

"This means that anyone who belongs to Christ has become a new person. The old life is gone, a new life has begun!"

2 CORINTHIANS 5:17

When you accept Jesus into your heart, you become a new person in Christ. On a daily basis, when you cooperate with the Holy Spirit, you will be transformed and renewed from the inside outward.

Submit to God your heart, mind, thoughts, and actions. Watch Him transform you! Old habits and desires will fade into oblivion as you dwell in the promises of God. Read the Bible and STAND on His promises. He will sustain you and equip you where ever He leads you!

Give God the glory!

Jennifer

Prayer Request

....

....

September 3

> "Jesus looked at them intently and said, 'Humanly speaking, it is impossible. But not with God. Everything is possible with God."
>
> **MARK 10: 27**

This verse is often quoted to encourage and strengthen fellow believers. In actuality, Jesus spoke these words to His disciples after there had been a discussion about who could be saved. There was a wealthy man who had inquired about what he needed to do to inherit eternal life: he had already obeyed the commandments of not committing murder, not committing adultery, not stealing, not cheating anyone, not testifying falsely, and had honored his parents. Jesus directed this wealthy man to sell all of his possessions and give the money to the poor, to which he responded by sadly walking away from Jesus. As the disciples began to question Jesus about who could be saved since it was "easier for a camel to go through the eye of a needle that a rich person to enter the kingdom of heaven", He responded to them with the scripture verse quoted above as our Verse of the Day.

So how does the response of Jesus to his disciples apply to us today as believers? I truly believe that this verse is rich with a promise: a promise that EVERYTHING is possible with God. Not some things, not many things, but EVERYTHING is possible with God. Even hope for a man who loved his possessions more than his living, breathing Savior. There's hope for each one of us, friend. Just trust Him.

Jennifer

Prayer Request

....

....

September 4

"The joy of the Lord is your strength."

NEHEMIAH 8:10

When was the last time you laughed? Really laughed out loud, deep from within your belly, eyes watering from laughing so hard? Afterwards I bet you felt terrific, didn't you? Laughter is excellent medicine.

Have you watched little children laugh? They think everything is hilarious and there are numerous statistics to show that when we are children, we laugh with more frequency than when we are adults. Perhaps it is because we "grow up" and become responsible. We all face difficult circumstances in our everyday lives but know this: God loves to hear you laugh! He made you and wants you to be filled with joy. When you laugh, you are acknowledging that you are alive, you are cheerful, and you are GRATEFUL for life. Show God how grateful you are that He gave your life and start giggling!

I'll ask it again: When was the last time you really laughed?

Jennifer

Prayer Request

September 5

"O Lord, You are my lamp. The Lord lights up my darkness."

2 SAMUEL 22:29

Are you in a dark place today? Are you depressed, discouraged, disheartened? You are not alone. The Lord promised us that he will never leave us nor forsake us (Hebrews 13:5, Deuteronomy 31:8, Isaiah 41:10-13).

Let the Lord shine His light into your dark place and guide you along the best path for your life. Take a moment right now to come to Him and ask Him for help. Often times you will hear someone say that they don't want to "bother" God with small, everyday situations but would rather only pray about "big" or complex situations. But God isn't just the solver of big problems, He is the solution for EVERY problem! As Christians, we are instructed to worry about nothing and pray about everything, thanking God for all he has done and telling him what we need. (Philippians 4:6-7)

When we pray, He listens to each one of us. You are a child of God. I know that He will provide a way for you. Let Him be the lamp for your darkness.

Be encouraged!

Jennifer

Prayer Request

....

....

September 6

> "Children obey your parents in everything, for this pleases the Lord."
>
> **COLOSSIANS 3:20**

Here's a newsflash: OBEY is not a four letter curse word! For every action, there is a reaction. Think about how our world would be impacted in a positive way if everyone chose to treat other people with respect, honor, and show integrity in all of their business and personal relationships.

In fact, obedience can actually be a blessing for both the person who is being obedient and the person who is the recipient of the obedience. Having said that, this does not mean that I am in any way encouraging someone to remain in a physically abusive situation or act as a "door mat" for abusive situations.

When you humble yourself and obey your parents, grandparents, boss, mentor, professor, etc., you are, in essence, honoring them. You are showing respect to their authority. And they, in turn, are responsible for how they treat you as well. Showing consistent, caring, and loving respect to others will make a huge impact in how you live your life. Live your best life today by honoring your parents.

Jennifer

Prayer Request

September 7

> "Why are your hearts filled with doubt? Look at my hands. Look at my feet. You can see that it's really me. Touch me and make sure that I am not a ghost, because ghosts don't have bodies as you see that I do."
>
> **LUKE 24:38-39**

Do you sometimes have doubts about the Lord, your salvation, His will for your life or His sovereignty? I encourage you to seek His face through reading your Bible and praying to Him. Knock on the door to His heart and He will answer you!

When we seek Him, the Lord will be found. If you're not close to Him, who moved? Ask Him to become your number one priority!

Jennifer

Prayer Request

....

....

September 8

"Those who exalt themselves will be humbled, and those who humble themselves will be exalted."

MATTHEW 23:12

Humbling yourself doesn't mean that you must become a doormat, allowing others to wipe their negativity/hostility/brutality on you. Humility is actually a sign of great strength.

Being humble is an act of servant leadership and shows a willing heart to serve others. When your heart is fully surrendered to the Lord, there is a natural tendency to genuinely want to serve others, showing them the same love that God has shown you. Unconditionally!

What actions can you modify in your own life to reflect the love of the Lord to others? How can you help someone in your own family? Neighborhood? Workplace? Church community?

When you are humble, you are never idle.

Jennifer

Prayer Request

September 9

"Trust in the Lord and do good. Then you will live safely in the land and prosper. Take delight in the Lord and He will give you the desires of your heart."

PROVERBS 37: 3-4

To me, delighting in the Lord is having the knowledge that my Savior loves me, no matter what. It is a consistent, abiding joy that dwells in each believer because we know that we are not home and the best is yet to come.

There are some people who assert that this scripture verse is quoted by believers who are motivated only for personal selfish gain, i.e. Delight in the Lord only to gain our own selfish desires.

However, if we are truly delighting in the Lord, our heart's desire will be to please Him and further His kingdom. In that sense, it is not selfish at all but rather an expression of gratitude to delight in Him and allow Him to give you the desires of your heart!

Jennifer

Prayer Request

....

....

September 10

"Now faith is the assurance of things hoped for, the conviction of things not seen."

HEBREWS 11:1

Faith is a common word with an uncommon result. Faith can move mountains! Just like muscles strengthen with exercise, our faith increases by exercising it.

Whatever situations you face, know this fact: God has you in the palm of His hand. Lean on Him, trust Him, and increase your faith. Grow those spiritual muscles and watch how your life will have more peace and joy.

Jennifer

Prayer Request

September 11

> "I praise You because I am fearfully and wonderfully made; Your works are wonderful, I know that full well."
>
> **PSALM 139:14**

The human body is a masterpiece. Our DNA makes us unique, one-of-a-kind, every detail handcrafted by God.

What causes us to think we are anything less than an incredible work of art by our Creator? Insecurities, comparing ourselves to others, and jealousy become thieves of our peace and threaten to rob us of our joy.

Know this fact: YOU. ARE. A. MASTERPIECE.

Jennifer

Prayer Request

....

....

September 12

> " For the eyes of the Lord range throughout the earth looking to strengthen the hearts fully committed to Him."
>
> **2 CHRONICLES 16:9**

I don't know about you but I want to be classified as someone who has a heart that is fully committed to the Lord!

When we are fully committed to something, we are "in it to win it", "sold out," "100 percent", etc. I think that there are times that we may believe that being committed to the Lord means that we have to be perfect, but that's not the truth. The truth is that He loves you exactly as you are today.

He wants our fully committed hearts, not the relentless pursuit of perfection. Give him your heart today. He will strengthen you.

Jennifer

Prayer Request

September 13

"The Lord will bless His people with peace."

PSALM 29:11

The pressures of life can leave us emotionally and physically drained. We may even believe that we are under equipped to juggle multiple responsibilities in our simple daily tasks.

How are some of the ways that people deal with the pressure? Overeating, overspending, overmedicating, and ultimately still being overwhelmed.

Take heart! As believers, we can look to our Lord for peace. Ask Him, Believe Him, Trust Him, and experience His PEACE.

Jennifer

Prayer Request

September 14

> "Blessed are all who hear the word of God and put it into practice."
>
> **LUKE 11:28**

Having a relationship with the Lord is the number one priority in my life. What about you?

Any kind of a quality relationship takes time and commitment to mature. Spending time with the Lord can become some of your most treasured moments of each day.

And then it is time to put what you've learned from Him into practice! Be the "hands and feet" of Jesus on earth as you minister to others. It is all about loving Him and serving others.

What has He called you to do? Do it, friend, do it!

Jennifer

Prayer Request

September 15

> "Behold, I have engraved you on the palms of my hands; your walls are continually before Me."
>
> **ISAIAH 49:16**

Do you ever write down action items in order to remember to do them? Perhaps you write these items on a sticky note, a notepad, or even on your hands? Yes, I used to be someone who had a habit of writing down important do-not-forget items on my hands in ink. While it was an annoying habit, I rarely forgot the items inscribed on my hands.

Do you know that the Lord has your name written on the palms of His hands? You are that important to Him that he has your name engraved on His hands. He loves you so!

Reach out to Him today and let Him know that you love Him.

Jennifer

Prayer Request

September 16

> "The steadfast love of the Lord never ceases; His mercies never end; they are new every morning; great is Your faithfulness."
>
> **LAMENTATIONS 3:22-23**

People can be fickle. Situations can drastically change in our health or finances. Jobs can terminate, friends can relocate, and even the weather can change in an instant.

No matter what you are facing, remember Who never changes, never waivers in His love for you. The Lord is faithful. I repeat, the Lord IS faithful and He never changes. He is with you today, tomorrow and for eternity.

Jennifer

Prayer Request

September 17

> " But the Holy Spirit produces this kind of fruit in our lives: love, joy, peace, patience, kindness, goodness, faithfulness, gentleness, and self-control."
>
> **GALATIANS 5:22**

Can you name someone in your life who exemplifies these qualities? How blessed you are to have them in your life! Most likely they are also a blessing to countless other people.

Contrary to what mainstream media may broadcast, the Bible is full of promises from God. When the Holy Spirit dwells in you as a believer, you are the recipient of all of the benefits of the Holy Spirit. Jesus said, "If you love me, you will obey my commandments. I will ask the Father, and He will give you another helper who will be with you forever. That helper is the Spirit of Truth. The world cannot accept Him, because it doesn't see or know Him. You know Him, because He lives with you and will be in you." John 14:15-17

Will you allow the Holy Spirit to guide your life? When you do, the "fruit" that you will produce will be beneficial to you and to others. Now go be AMAZING!

Jennifer

Prayer Request

....

....

September 18

"Because of Christ and our faith in Him, we can come boldly and confidently into God's presence."

EPHESIANS 3:12

Scripture assures us that we can come "boldly and confidently" into the presence of God. Boldness is defined as "willing to take risks or act innovatively." Confidence is defined as "the state of feeling certain about the truth of something."

When we accept the truth that we can come into God's presence with boldness and confidence, it changes everything about our prayer life! Boldly and confidently approach the Lord with your prayers, petitions, and praise.

Jennifer

Prayer Request

September 19

"God is obviously with you, helping
you in everything you do."

GENESIS 21:22

When Ambimelech uttered these words to Abraham, it was the truth. God was with Abraham. And we know that Abraham was promised by God that he would become a great and mighty nation, and that all the nations of the earth would be blessed through him. (Genesis 18:17)

The promises spoken to Abraham are our inherited promises through our faith. Take comfort, friend, and know that God is with you in everything you do. He will not leave you nor will He abandon you.

Jennifer

Prayer Request

September 20

"It is not by force nor by strength, but by My Spirit, says the Lord of Heaven's Armies."

ZECHARIAH 4: 6

An angel of the Lord interpreted a vision for Zechariah specifically regarding the rebuilding of the temple in Jerusalem, which was a task that had been undertaken by a man named Zerubbabel. Zerubbabel faced challenges but was encouraged by the prophets. If you want more details about the rebuilding of the temple by Zerubbabel or the various visions of Zechariah, I encourage you to read the book of Zechariah.

How is this word of encouragement applicable to us today? First of all, know this fact: God is the same yesterday, today, and tomorrow. He doesn't change, He doesn't lie, and He is steadfast.

The same Spirit of God exists, removing those mountains of doubt in your life, expelling discouragement from your heart, removing financial obstacles from your household, providing physical strength to your body, instilling mental clarity in your emotions, and loving you as a uniquely designed individual.

You are a masterpiece, designed for a purpose!

Jennifer

Prayer Request

September 21

> "The Spirit of the Sovereign Lord is upon me, and the Lord has anointed me to bring good news to the poor. He has sent me to comfort the brokenhearted and to proclaim that captives will be released, and prisoners will be freed. He has sent me to tell those who mourn that the time of the Lord's favor has come, and with it, the day of God's anger against their enemies."
>
> **ISAIAH 61: 1-2**

Are you in a virtual prison? Are you chained to doubt, insecurity, or guilt? Are you shackled to regret, despair or depression? What is weighing you down or causing you to feel burdened with remorse?

Today is a new day and I encourage you to embrace the future that the Lord has created for you. Seek the Lord and believe that He wants good for you, not evil. The time of mourning is over and the time to LIVE is now.

You were not created to carry your burdens alone and He wants to help you.

Jennifer

Prayer Request

September 22

> "For the Lord grants wisdom! From His mouth comes knowledge and understanding."
>
> **PROVERBS 2:6**

If you ever wondered how to begin reading the Bible on a daily basis, I encourage you to consider starting with the book of Proverbs, one chapter a day. There are 31 chapters and you could easily finish the book of Proverbs within one month of daily reading.

Proverbs is full of so much more than wonderful quotes because it contains actual knowledge and wisdom. Take some time today to start reading a chapter a day.

Pray that God would open your mind and your heart as you read scripture. Wisdom is God-given and I encourage you to ASK and SEEK it!

Jennifer

Prayer Request

September 23

> "For I hold you by your right hand – I, the Lord your God. And I say to you, "Don't be afraid. I am here to help you."
>
> **ISAIAH 41:13**

What giants are you facing today? A bad medical report, financial distress, relationship woes? Apply this scripture to whatever your situation is and know that God means what He says so believe Him. HE is here to help you. Let Him guide you through every decision, every relationship, and every battle. He is not a liar and His word never fails.

I'll repeat it. He means what He says. Don't be afraid because HE will help you.

Jennifer

Prayer Request

....

....

September 24

> "I have spoken and I will bring it to pass;
> I have purposed and I will do it."
>
> **ISAIAH 46:8-11**

What has God spoken to your heart? What promises are you believing will come to fruition?

There is an acronym the I love: P.U.S.H. Pray Until Something Happens. Are you pushing?

1. When you are faced with a mountain of despair, keep pushing.
2. When you are in the midst of a financial crisis, keep pushing.
3. When you are uncertain as to your future, keep pushing.
4. When you want to give up, keep pushing.

Do this: Pray until something happens!

If God said it, He meant it. He will bring it to pass, but you must believe Him. He is faithful to complete what He started in you.

Jennifer

Prayer Request

September 25

"I can do all things through Christ who gives me strength."

PHILIPPIANS 4:13

Do you need supernatural strength for the giants you are facing? Is it a giant of discouragement? Is it a giant of mediocrity? Is it a giant of family issues? Is it a giant of laziness or compromise?

Surrender your plans to the Lord and allow Him to give you His strength. When you trade your strength for His strength, those "giants" will fall! Believe what He says about you and believe that He can do the impossible in your life.

Jennifer

Prayer Request

September 26

"But if we HOPE for what we do not see, we wait for it with patience."

ROMANS 8:25

What are you praying for in your life or in the life of another person? What are you believing to happen? In what areas are you earnestly seeking God to intervene or act on your behalf? Do your prayers line up with God's sovereign will?

Keep praying and keep earnestly seeking His will for your life. Time is precious and any time spent seeking the will of God through prayer is never wasted.

Jennifer

Prayer Request

September 27

> "If we confess our sins, He is faithful and just to forgive us and cleanse us from all our unrighteousness."
>
> **1 JOHN 1:9**

Is some sin weighing on your heart or your conscience? Confess it today to the Lord. He is faithful to hear you and will forgive you.

Reach out to Him today through prayer. Tell Him your thoughts, concerns, burdens, and know that He is there for you.

When you humble yourself in the sight of the Lord, He will forgive you and set you on your feet on solid rock again. He never fails us.

Jennifer

Prayer Request

....

....

September 28

> "If any of you lacks wisdom, let him ask of God, who gives to all liberally and without reproach, and it will be given to him."
>
> **JAMES 1:5**

Do you need wisdom in a certain area of your life? Is it hard for you to ask for help? Do you believe that if you ask for help that you would be considered weak or incompetent? Perhaps you were raised in a home where being self-sufficient was highly praised? Or maybe you were told that being too inquisitive could be interpreted as rude? Or have you ever asked a question and sincerely wanted a truthful answer, only to be met with a sarcastic remark such as "Duh?" Don't let the rudeness and insecurity of others dampen your desire to seek wisdom. Keep on seeking wisdom!

Friend, there are no dumb or silly questions to God. If you need wisdom in a certain area, ASK Him! He loves you and He is on your team. He cares deeply for you and you are His child. Let me ask you again. Do you need wisdom in a certain area? ASK Him. He will answer you.

Jennifer

Prayer Request

September 29

"Rejoice always, pray continually, give thanks in all circumstances, for this is God's will in Christ Jesus for you."

1 THESSALONIANS 5:16-18

Are you a loud person or a quiet person? I tend to be a loud person but there are certain seasons in my life where I have gravitated towards being a quiet person. In my loud voice and in my quiet voice, I can still praise God. And you can, too.

Sometimes I sing, whistle, clap my hands, hum, dance, twirl, and/or laugh. Other times I am quietly reverent and down on my knees whispering my praise and prayers. Sometimes I clean my house and sing praise songs at the top of my voice. I will whistle praise songs while I'm on my kayak or hiking on a trail. Other times I will just smile, remembering how faithful the Lord has been during my life and I will simply utter the words, "Thank you, thank you, thank you."

Friend, regardless of HOW you praise the Lord, just DO IT! He is worthy!

Jennifer

Prayer Request

....

....

September 30

"But THANKS be to God,! He gives us the victory through our Lord Jesus Christ."

1 CORINTHIANS 15:57

When was the last time you grumbled about your circumstances, your job, your finances, or your family members? Be honest! If I'm honest, I grumbled just last night to a friend about a specific circumstance in my life. And woke up this morning thinking about it all over again, replaying it as I started the day. And the root of the problem was my utter lack of gratitude.

Is that God's will for us as believers? No!

What is the answer to being ungrateful? Giving THANKS to God for everything He has blessed us with in our lives. And watch how those blessings grow!

Jennifer

Prayer Request

OCTOBER

"To all who mourn in Israel, He will give you a crown of beauty for ashes, a joyous blessing instead of mourning, festive praise instead of despair."

Isaiah 61:3

October 1

"To all who mourn in Israel, He will give you a crown of beauty for ashes, a joyous blessing instead of mourning, festive praise instead of despair."

ISAIAH 61:3

Many years ago, one manner in which someone showed that they were in mourning was to dress in sackcloth and cover themselves with ashes. While we may not demonstrate our grief in that same way today, we do still grieve deeply for the loss of someone.

What or whom are you mourning today? What person, event, or situation is causing you grief? Give it to the Lord and let Him give you BEAUTY for the "ashes" in which you've covered yourself. It's time to move forward into the abundant life He has planned for you.

Jennifer

Prayer Request

October 2

> "Keep on asking, and you will receive what you ask for, keep on seeking and you will find. Keep on knocking and the door will be opened to you. For everyone who asks, receives. Everyone who seeks, funds. Everyone who knocks, the door will be opened to you."
>
> **MATTHEW 7:7-8**

What have you been praying for to happen in your life or in the life of a loved one? Have you been asking God about it for such a long time? Is what you're asking for in alignment with the will of God?

Keep asking, keep seeking His will, and keep knocking on that door. He hears you.

His timing isn't our timing and it's our human nature to be impatient. Trust Him and His perfect timing today in your situation. Keep your chin up and your heart open to receive His answers for you.

Jennifer

Prayer Request

....

....

October 3

"Commit your actions to the Lord,
and your plans will succeed."

PROVERBS 16:3

"What do you do for a living?" is a common question asked when getting to know someone for the first time. We frequently define ourselves by our professions, our hobbies, our children, our marital status, our social media ratings, and even our age group.

The most important question I think we should ask ourselves is, "How does God see me?" and "Who does HE say I am?" You are redeemed. You are valued. You are worthy. You have been called. You are the apple of His eye. You are chosen.

When you know WHO you are in Christ, you are truly prepared to do HIS work on this earth. And when you commit your plans to Him, you will succeed.

Jennifer

Prayer Request

October 4

"How good and pleasant it is when
God's people live together in unity!"

PSALM 133:1

As believers, we are called to set an example of God's love to the world. And it should start in our homes, in our relationships, and with other believers.

"A house divided cannot stand" is a quote that I have heard all of my life. Although I heard it as it relates to sports, I think it can apply to us as Christians.

Follow Christ's example: Exemplify the love you want to see in others. Unite with other believers and proclaim the Good News to the entire world.

Jennifer

Prayer Request

October 5

> "Don't you realize that your body is the temple of the Holy Spirit, who lives in you and was given to you by God? You do not belong to yourself, for God bought you with a high price. So you must honor God with your body."
>
> **1 CORINTHIANS 6:19-20**

I attended a faith-based elementary and high school. Religion class was a part of our daily curriculum. I always heard this scripture used in specific reference to maintaining sexual purity; however, it can be expanded to be applicable to every area of our lives: sexual purity, eating habits, exercise routines, clothing choices, mental health, etc..

Friend, your body is not a garbage dump! Quit feeding it tons of junk food. Quit watching trashy television and then expecting your overall mood to be enlightened. It doesn't work out that way.

1. Consider your exercise routine. Do you have one yet?
2. Are you surrounding yourself with positive people or negative influences?
3. Are your conversations filled with anger, sarcasm, gossip, bitterness or do you use life-giving words?
4. What kind of music are you listening to on a regular basis?

Trash in equals trash out. Again, you are not a garbage dump!

Jennifer

Prayer Request

October 6

"Pray for one another."

JAMES 5:16

This scripture is powerful. As believers, we have been instructed to pray for one another. I encourage you to take this to heart. Prayer is action!

When I tell someone that I'm praying for them, I mean it. I take their concerns to the Lord and ask for His will to be done. One of the ways I remember to pray for specific individuals is a dry erase board in my prayer area. I have kept a prayer journal in the past and I also have various prayer boxes with specific prayers for people written on slips of paper. I also will text or email the prayer I'm praying for specific individuals back to them so that we are in agreement on their request. Prayer is simple but it IS effective.

Here's the bottom line: PRAY for others. In addition to prayer, help meet their specific physical needs if possible. Deliver food, pick up their groceries or medicine from the pharmacy for them, visit with them, write them encouraging messages on postcards, donate clothing to them, or bring them to church with you. And still PRAY for them. Intercede on their behalf and pray, pray, pray. Prayer works!

Jennifer

Prayer Request

October 7

"But as for me and my house, we will serve the Lord."

JOSHUA 24:15

What or whom are you serving today? Ask yourself, where do you spend your time, your finances, and your energy? What movies are you watching, what books are you reading, and what songs are you singing? With whom do you spend time with on a regular and consistent basis?

It is wonderful to have romantic relationships, hobbies, career opportunities, friendships, but remember whom you serve as a believer in Jesus Christ. Your devotion, your gratitude, and your very life itself belongs to the Lord.

Serve Him with your whole heart and watch Him truly bless you.

Jennifer

Prayer Request

....

....

October 8

> "I will also tell you this: If two of you agree here on earth concerning anything you ask, my Father in heaven will do it for you. For where two or three gather together as my followers, I am there among them."
>
> **MATTHEW 18:19**

There is POWER when believers come together for prayer. Who are your fellow believers with whom you pray with for your needs and their needs?

Need some encouragement? I promise if you shift the focus from yourself to helping others, your burdens will seem lighter. Lift one another up in prayer, help each other daily, and pray together in one accord. Your lifestyle will reflect the most sincere devotions of your heart. Pursue the Lord with your whole heart and your whole being. He is worth it!

Jennifer

Prayer Request

October 9

"Do not fear, for I have redeemed you. I have called you by name. You are Mine."

ISAIAH 43:1-2

Do you know that God loves you? Before you answer that with a casual shrug or a quick of course, reflect on what I'm asking you. Do you know that He loves you?

We can be assured that He loves us and that He loves us deeply. He created each one of us and called us by our name. He says that we belong to Him and He means it.

Know that you are loved by your Creator.

Jennifer

Prayer Request

October 10

"Give all your worries and cares to God, for He cares about you."

1 PETER 5:7

What keeps you awake at night? Do you count sheep or do you talk to The Shepherd?

When you are worried about something, do you get on the phone to call a friend or do you talk to Your Greatest Friend?

With whom do you share your concerns with on a regular basis? Is it your friends, family, or co-workers? While it is wonderful to have a strong support system, remember to share your concerns with the One who loves you the most and the One who uniquely designed you.

The Lord is ready and willing to listen to you today!

Jennifer

Prayer Request

October 11

"Behold, I am the Lord, the God of all flesh. Is anything too hard for me?"

JEREMIAH 32:27

A valley of dry bones came to life at His command. Do you believe this? I repeat, do you truly believe this promise from the Lord? He can resurrect any dead dream within you.

Whatever problem you're facing, whatever situation you're dealing with, know that nothing is too difficult for Him. Absolutely NOTHING!

If God says it, He will do it. Pray, trust, and believe that He is guiding your life. When you pray according to His will and surrender your plans to His plans, watch out!

Miracles are on the way!

Jennifer

Prayer Request

October 12

'Your roots will grow down into God's love and keep you strong. And may you have the power to understand, as all God's people should, how wide, how long, how high, and how deep His love is."

EPHESIANS 3:17-18

God's love is steadfast. Unlike the favor of people, God's love is never fickle.

HE IS WITH YOU.

Even now, even in the midst of uncertainty in our chaotic world, He still sits on the throne. He is in total control and He has a plan. Do not despair about world events.

When God says that He loves you, He means it. When He says that His love is long and wide and we cannot possibly comprehend the depths of it, He means it! HE is Lord of all and He loves each one of us.

Jennifer

Prayer Request

October 13

> "I will climb up to my watchtower and stand at my guard post. There I will wait to see what the Lord says and how He will answer my complaint."
>
> **HABAKKUK 2:1**

When you are upset, worried, or frustrated, what do you do? Do you fret silently, clenching your teeth and shaking your head at the situation? Do you call your friends and vent to them? Do you self-medicate, overeat or overthink the situation?

Take your issue directly to the Lord. Speak to Him. He is listening and He cares about every situation in your life. Wait on Him and watch Him work in your situation. He is omniscient. His word never fails.

Jennifer

Prayer Request

. . . .

. . . .

October 14

"Do not be quickly provoked in your spirit
for anger resides in the lap of fools."

ECCLESIASTES 7:9

Anger is defined by Webster's Dictionary as "a violent passion of the mind excited by a real or supposed injury; usually accompanied with a propensity to take vengeance, or to obtain satisfaction from the offending party."

As believers, we may face daily challenges in which it seems difficult, if not impossible, to respond to others with love and compassion. It may also seem unfair to not respond with anger, especially when we feel that we are entitled to hold on to anger against someone who has intentionally caused us harm.

I have heard it said that the person who holds onto anger against someone is like drinking poison and expecting the other person to die. Choosing to no longer be angry doesn't just happen by chance. You must make the decision to no longer be angry and thereby opening up the opportunity for forgiveness. Step by step, little by little, your heart will begin to heal.

Follow the wisdom of this scripture verse and don't be foolish. Allow yourself to be free from anger today!

Jennifer

Prayer Request

October 15

> "In Him we have redemption through His blood, the forgiveness for our trespasses, according to the riches of His GRACE."
>
> **EPHESIANS 1:7**

Grace.

A simple word with a profound impact. When Jesus died on the cross, He bore our sins with Him. No more sacrifice needed for atonement for our sins through the shedding of blood from bulls, rams, goats, and other animals.

HE WAS THE ULTIMATE SACRIFICE.

And as a result of His resurrection, we have a new covenant with the Lord. When we become Christian believers, we have been redeemed through the blood of His sacrifice. Our sins have been forgiven. We don't deserve it and there is nothing we can do to earn it. It is through grace. Sweet, simple, and beautiful grace.

What you have received, freely give. grace to you, friends!

Jennifer

Prayer Request

. . . .

. . . .

October 16

> "She is energetic and strong, a hard worker.
> She makes sure her dealings are profitable;
> her lamp burns late into the night."
>
> **PROVERBS 31:17**

Having a good work ethic is a wonderful characteristic for us to possess; however, the overall description of a "Proverbs 31 woman" seems almost impossible for anyone to obtain!

If you continue reading the rest of Proverbs 31, you will see a description of a woman who spins thread, helps the poor, is an early riser, makes her own clothes, dresses in beautiful clothes, respects her husband, laughs at the future, has no fear, has children who bless her, purchases land, plants a vineyard, and is a merchant who creates her own garments.

Don't let this scripture discourage you in thinking that a Proverbs 31 woman is someone in relentless pursuit of perfection because it is not meant to be taken in that manner. Nope, not at all!

Let Proverbs 31 inspire and encourage you in knowing that you have the ability to set the standard for excellence for your entire family and for many future generations.

So be excellent, my female friends. And to my male friends, treasure your wife! She is truly a gift from God.

Jennifer

Prayer Request

October 17

"Do not be afraid, for I am with you."

ISAIAH 41:10

We are instructed to not be afraid/do not fear approximately 365 times in scripture. That's a "Do not fear" for each day of the year!

My friend, what causes you to fear? What causes you anxiety? Pick your favorite "Do not Verse" and apply it for every day of the year.

DO NOT FEAR. Give it to God. He's got you and He will never leave you.

Jennifer

Prayer Request

October 18

"Be still and know that I am God."

PSALM 46:10

There are times to actively pursue whatever God has placed on your heart and then there are times to just be still.

Being still doesn't mean being lazy or complacent. It also doesn't mean sitting idly by while someone else does the hard work for you.

Learn to be sensitive to the leading of the Lord's direction. Pray. Trust. Listen.

Rest in the knowledge that God loves you. He is not against you. He is for you and He wants the best for you.

Jennifer

Prayer Request

October 19

> "Look after each other so that none of you fails to receive the grace of God. Watch out that no poisonous root of bitterness grows up to trouble you, corrupting many."
>
> **HEBREWS 12:15**

Look after each other! As believers we are called to encourage and edify one another.

Today is the day to release any bitterness or unforgiveness towards your family or friends. Is this going to be an easy process? No, but take the first step by praying for assistance from the Holy Spirit to forgive those who have hurt you.

And then follow the leading of the Lord in removing the bitter roots in your own heart. Let the bitterness go and watch God plant beautiful seeds of victory in your life.

Jennifer

Prayer Request

....

....

October 20

> "I have seen what they do, but I will heal them anyway! I will lead them. I will comfort those who mourn, bringing words of praise to their lips."
>
> **ISAIAH 57:18**

Thankfully, the Lord loves us despite our actions, attitudes, and behaviors. He is with us as we encounter daily struggles and receive opportunities for growth.

He is faithful and He is worthy of praise. He brings comfort and solace to the broken hearted and He is ever present in times of trouble.

What a comfort to know that our Creator loves us not because of WHAT we do but because of WHO He is as our Risen Savior!

Jennifer

Prayer Request

....

....

October 21

"The Lord is my strength and my song;
He has given me VICTORY!"

EXODUS 15:2

Whatever season you are in right now, know that God is for you, not against you. He has the best plan for your life and surrendering your own plan to Him will result in Victory. He always wins and His word never fails or returns void.

Isn't it comforting to know that He wants only good for you all the days of your life? Give Him some praise and get ready for your Victory!

Jennifer

Prayer Request

October 22

> "He will cover you with His feathers; He will shelter you with His wings. His faithful promises are your armor and protection."
>
> **PSALM 91:4**

After a forest fire, some park rangers were walking among the debris. One of them saw a petrified bird huddled on the ground, mummified and charred from the fire. He touched it with his boot, and underneath the dead body of the bird were several baby chicks, very much alive! The mother bird literally spread her wings to shelter her babies from the blazing fire, sacrificing her life to protect her babies.

Likewise, Our Heavenly Father shelters us with His wings of protection. His faithful promises are in scripture. And these promises shield us from the enemy.

Whatever "fire" surrounds you today, use your spiritual weapons to defend yourself and your loved ones. When you remain on your knees in prayer, you will stand on His praises!

Jennifer

Prayer Request

October 23

> "A man of many companions may suffer ruin, but there is a friend who sticks closer than a brother."
>
> **PSALM 18:24**

Friends are like jewels: some are sparkly and fun, some are brilliant, some are dull, some are hardened and uncomfortable, some seem to hang around our neck and wear us out, and some are just the right fit.

What kind of friend are you? Learn how to be the best kind of friend: one who models themselves after Jesus. He sticks "closer than a brother" to us.

When our hearts are aligned with His heart, our motives are pure and unselfish. Learn to truly love and cherish the friends you have in your life.

Jennifer

Prayer Request

....

....

October 24

> "I press on to reach the end of the race and receive the heavenly prize for which God, through Jesus Christ, is calling us."
>
> **PHILIPPIANS 3:14**

We are in a race, a long distance marathon, commonly referred to as LIFE. How are you living your life? Are you seeking God's direction daily? What long and short term goals do you have for yourself, your family, your team at work?

There are a few absolutely certain things in LIFE and one of those things is that our LIFE will end one day. When you have completed your LIFE Marathon, what do you hope to have accomplished for the Kingdom of God?

Has the Lord called you to write a book, learn to play a musical instrument, become more healthy, go back to school, build an orphanage, become a missionary, be kind to an elderly neighbor, adopt a child, start a business, become a physician, build a house, travel to a foreign country, become a teacher, start a non-profit? What is it that He has called you to do?

Friend, it's time to get busy. If He has called you to do something for His Kingdom, quit stalling. Pray for direction and know that if He has called you to it, He will equip you.

Jennifer

Prayer Request

October 25

"Live peacefully with each other."

1 THESSALONIANS 5:13

Are you living in harmony with your immediate family? Are you at peace with your extended family? How about your interactions with your co-workers? Are you a true friend to your friends?

Take a moment today and examine all of your relationships. Constant strife and struggles are not a way to live in peace. Protect your peace.

Believe it or not, it IS possible to live with, be friends with, and work with people who have different beliefs and values than you. This doesn't mean that you have to adopt their belief system or "water down" your own opinions.

There is great strength is remaining calm, accepting and loving people for who they are as fellow human beings created by God. When in conflict, it is wise to show restraint when necessary, use basic good manners, listen to others, and be kind. Not every negative thought that pops in your head needs to be expressed! You have two ears and one mouth. Listen more, talk less.

It simply means this: Be at PEACE with others.

Jennifer

Prayer Request

October 26

"A gentle answer turns away wrath, but
a harsh word stirs up anger."

PROVERBS 15:1

Are you ever presented with situations where people are irritable, ignorant, or just plain irate? I know that I personally encounter multiple situations in which I am faced with a choice to respond in anger or in love. The best way for me to maintain my composure is to dwell on the scriptures and know that God loves everyone.

Yes, He loves everyone!

Be gentle with others and watch how your relationships with others will improve dramatically. The Lord instructs us to live in peace.

Jennifer

Prayer Request

October 27

"But now ask and keep on asking and you will receive,
so that your JOY may be full and complete."

JOHN 16:24

Keep on asking and keep on believing that God wants to bless you! Ask, keep on asking, and believe that He will fill you with His joy, peace, and love.

A significant part of the JOY we will receive, will come from the difficult times in which we had to earnestly seek the wisdom and counsel of the Lord. Seek Him and His answers for the questions and concerns in your life.

He wants to help you and fill you with his JOY!

Jennifer

Prayer Request

October 28

> "But you are not controlled by your sinful nature. You are controlled by the Spirit if you have the Spirit of God living in you."
>
> **ROMANS 8:9**

Control.

It's a word we hear often in different contexts: self-control, parental control, governmental control, even a remote control.

Whom or what controls you? Your friends? Your parents? The television programs you watch?

As a believer, we are controlled by the Holy Spirit when we fully surrender our lives to the Lord.

Cast aside all doubt that you can give up bad habits or poor decisions. You can do it with the help of the Lord. He wants to bless you as you trust Him with every area of your life.

Jennifer

Prayer Request

October 29

"When God's people are in need, be ready to help them. Always be EAGER to practice hospitality."

ROMANS 12:13

Welcoming others to my home is a normal routine and a vital part of the way that I was raised. In the South, we know how to host parties and make people feel welcome in our homes! Typically, the people we welcome into our homes are friends, family and acquaintances.

Compare that to making anyone feel welcome in your home. Ask yourself, would you invite total strangers to your home for a "meet and greet" with your neighbor? Would you willingly extend an offer of fellowship to that lonely person at your office, school, church, or gym? Would you be willing to host a bible study in your home?

Think about ways you can practice out-of-the-box hospitality to others!

Jennifer

Prayer Request

October 30

> "But now this what the Lord says: Do not weep any longer for I will reward you, says the Lord. Your children will come back to you from the distant land of the enemy."
>
> **JEREMIAH 31:16**

Do you have children? If so, I'm sure you provide all of their basic needs: food, shelter, clothing, healthcare, transportation, and education. You most likely even provide the "extras" of sporting activities, hobbies, electronic devices, and vacations.

When was the last time you prayed for your child? Not just a hurried "bless him/her after a sneeze" kind of prayer but a thoughtful, strategic prayer for your child's life? Your child needs the protection of your prayers in every area of his/her life.

There are so many influences surrounding our children. Let YOUR influence be the shining example of a parent who seeks after God with all of your heart!

Jennifer

Prayer Request

October 31

> "For I hold you by your right hand- I, the Lord, your God. And I say to you, Don't be afraid. I am here to help you."
>
> **ISAIAH 41:13**

The majority of us are right handed. Have you ever tried to perform daily functions with your dominant hand tied behind your back? If you were doing it as a dare or a challenge in a skit, it would be comical to watch you try to feed yourself, comb your hair, brush your teeth, or put on makeup with your non-dominant hand.

In the alternative, when someone holds our right hand, we are also unable to use it as our dominant hand. Once again we find ourselves powerless to write, feed ourselves, comb our hair, brush our teeth, type, write a letter, but the difference is we are guided by the person holding our hand. They are leading us as we trust them.

When the Lord says that He is holding our right hand, let Him! What a relief to know that He tells us to not be afraid because He has our right hand. He is leading us and guiding us on the best path for our lives.

Jennifer

Prayer Request

NOVEMBER

"Love does not delight in evil but rejoices with the truth. It always protects, always trusts, always hopes, always perseveres. Love never fails."

1 Corinthians 13:1

November 1

"Love does not delight in evil but rejoices with the truth. It always protects, always trusts, always hopes, always perseveres. Love never fails."

1 CORINTHIANS 13:1

Are there people in your life whom you find difficult to love? If so, I recommend reading that scripture verse and applying it to your situation. Is it easy to love unconditionally? No. Is it scriptural? Yes. How do we apply this on a daily basis? Love the Lord and love others as yourself.

Love never fails. Take that verse and hide it in your heart.

Jennifer

Prayer Request

November 2

> "He will cover you with His feathers. He will shelter you with His wings. His faithful promises are your armor and protection."
>
> **PSALM 91:4**

I encourage you to reflect on how the Lord has been faithful to you and your family. If you're reading this, you're still alive! And if you're alive, God has a plan and a purpose for your life. You are here for a reason.

Friend, rejoice in the fact that God sees you and He loves you. He will cover you with His feathers and protect you with His wings.

He's got you covered and He is faithful. Rest easy.

Jennifer

Prayer Request

....

....

November 3

> "Look up into the heavens. Who created all the stars? He brings them out like an army, one after another, calling each by its name. Because of His great power and incomparable strength, not a single one is missing."
>
> **ISAIAH 40:26**

God is powerful. He created everything and gave it a name. each one of us is a masterpiece, perfectly designed by God for a unique purpose.

Are you aware of how special you are to the Lord? He designed you! You are a masterpiece.

Friend, talk to the Lord about finding your purpose. Ask Him to reveal what His plan is for your life. Get in agreement with Him and watch Him show you how to fulfill your purpose on this earth.

Jennifer

Prayer Request

....

....

November 4

"It is good to give thanks to the Lord, to sing praises to the Most High. It is good to proclaim your UNFAILING love in the morning, Your faithfulness in the evening."

PSALM 92:1-2

Have you ever been betrayed by a friend or loved one? Been talked about, whispered about, lied about in the workplace or in your social circle? It happens to all of us.

When our family members, friends, or colleagues fail us, know this fact: The Lord will stick close to you. He is consistent. He is loyal. He is faithful.

His love never fails.

Start your day with excitement!

Jennifer

Prayer Request

November 5

> "Let's not get tired of doing what is good. At just the right time we will REAP a HARVEST of blessing if we don't give up."
>
> **GALATIANS 6:9**

How many times have you heard the saying, "You will reap what you sow?" It is the absolute truth.

Keep doing good, even when no one is watching, no one is handing out awards, no one is dedicating a building in your name, and no one is donating money to charitable causes in your name.

Keep. Doing. Good.

God sees you! HE knows. And He will reward you.

Jennifer

Prayer Request

....

....

November 6

"I lift my eyes up to the hills, where does my help come from? My help comes from the Lord, maker of heaven and earth. Indeed, He who watches over Israel neither slumbers nor sleeps."

PSALM 121: 1

Those words are powerful because it clearly identifies for us as to where we should seek our help in times of trouble. Our first inclination may be to run to self-help books or to "phone a friend" but we should lift our eyes and hearts to the Lord FIRST before we involve others.

Pray about every situation and ask for clarity. Lift your eyes to the One who cares for you. He's got you covered.

Jennifer

Prayer Request

November 7

> "Be anxious for nothing, but in everything by prayer and supplication with thanksgiving, let your requests be made known to God. And the peace of God, which passes all understanding will guard your hearts and your minds in Christ Jesus."
>
> **PHILIPPIANS 4:6-7**

What is causing you anxiety? What is weighing on your heart? What keeps you awake at night?

Friend, whatever "it" is, give it to God. Pray about it and then release "it" to His care. He has the plan for your life and it is a good plan for your future. Allow Him to guide you and develop the peace in your heart to pass all understanding. He is faithful and consistent.

Jennifer

Prayer Request

....

....

November 8

"My child, pay attention to what I say. Listen carefully to My words. Do not let them out of your sight, keep them within your heart."

PROVERBS 4:20-21

We are each given two ears and one mouth. It's for a reason!

1. When the Lord instructs us to listen, He means it.
2. When He tells us to keep them in our sight, He is directing us to follow His guidelines for life.
3. When He tells us to treasure His words in our hearts, do it, friend.

Listen, follow, and keep His word in your heart!

Jennifer

Prayer Request

November 9

> "In the last days, God says, I will pour out my Spirit upon all people. Your sons and daughters will prophesy. Your young men will see visions, and your old men will dream dreams. In those days I will pour out my Spirit even on my servants-men and women alike- and they will prophesy. And I will cause wonders in the heavens above and signs on the earth below-blood and fire and clouds of smoke. The sun will become dark and the moon will turn blood red before that great and glorious day of the Lord arrives. But everyone who calls upon the name of the Lord will be saved."
>
> **ACTS 2:17-21**

It's simple but profound: Call upon the name of the Lord and be saved. Call out to Him today!

When we call out to Him, we are submitting ourselves to His sovereignty. We are acknowledging that He is the source of our strength and He will deliver us. Have you acknowledged Him as the Lord of your life?

Have a great day as you acknowledge that His Spirit goes with you.

Jennifer

Prayer Request

....

....

November 10

> "All your children will be taught by the Lord, and great will be their peace."
>
> **ISAIAH 54:13**

Great will be your PEACE. The world may be in a state of chaos but there is PEACE in Jesus.

Raising children is not easy and it is not for the faint of heart. But there is a helper – the Holy Spirit!

Do you want your parenting skills to have an eternal impact on your children? If so, invite the Holy Spirit into your home and into your parenting interactions with your children.

Pray for guidance. It will be time well spent when you pray for direction and guidance of the Lord.

Jennifer

Prayer Request

November 11

"Thank the Lord! Praise His name! Tell the nations what He has done. Let them all know how mighty He is!"

ISAIAH 12:4

What has the Lord done for you? What has He done in the lives of your loved ones? I promise you that if you dig deep, you'll find something that He has done in your life for which you should be incredibly grateful.

Today, I challenge you to shift your perspective from focusing on what you don't have to what you DO have. Remember to be grateful.

Praise God and tell others what He has done in YOUR life! He is worthy to be praised.

Jennifer

Prayer Request

November 12

> "What then, can we say in response to such things? God is for us, who can be against us?"
>
> **ROMANS 8:31**

Whom or What is coming against you today? Your own negative thoughts, a person who seeks to harm you, a difficult situation at work, or a strained relationship with a loved one? What is your IT?

I encourage you to name whatever IT is and then repeat Romans 8:31. It cannot stand against the love and power of Jesus Christ.

Know this fact: God is for you! You are an Overcomer. Start living like you believe it!

Jennifer

Prayer Request

November 13

> "For I know the plans I have for you, says the Lord. They are plans of good and not for disaster, to give you a future and a hope. In those days when you pray, I will listen. If you look for me wholeheartedly, you will find me."
>
> **JEREMIAH 29:11-13**

Do you know that God is FOR you? He is not against you! Too often we hear stories of people raised in homes where they were made to feel that God is against them, wanting them to feel ashamed or scared. When you really know God, you know that He wants a relationship with you. He wants your heart-all of it!

Know this, friend: HE LOVES YOU. He is your biggest fan!

He created and designed you for a purpose. Start believing it!

Jennifer

Prayer Request

November 14

"But whenever someone turns to the Lord, the veil is taken away. For the Lord is the Spirit, and wherever the Spirit of the Lord is, there is FREEDOM."

2 CORINTHIANS 3:16-17

Has someone shared the Gospel with you? Most likely there has been at least one person, either face-to-face, via television, via radio, via the internet, who has previously told you that God loves you and sent His son to die for you. However, if no one has ever told you about the Lord, take a moment and read John 3:16. If you don't have a bible, google that verse.

Let this sink into your spirit today: GOD LOVES YOU.

He. LOVES. You. Period.

And wherever the Spirit of the Lord exists, there is true freedom. He loves you exactly as you are and exactly where you are right now in your life journey. He wants a relationship with you. I encourage you to take a moment now to spend some time with Him. Thank Him and Praise Him!

Jennifer

Prayer Request

November 15

"Yes, I am the vine; you are the branches. Those who remain in Me, and I in them, will produce much fruit. For apart from Me, you can do nothing."

JOHN 15:5

Remaining in God's word is so vital to our daily walk with Him. The "fruit" you produce will be plentiful when you allow Him to direct your life.

Challenges and obstacles will come, but know that you will not merely survive-you will thrive when you remain in Him. Your life will become the most productive and fulfilling when you abide in the true Vine.

Jennifer

Prayer Request

November 16

> Jesus replied, "You must love the Lord your God
> with all your heart, all your soul, and all your mind.
> This is the first and greatest commandment."
>
> **MATTHEW 22:37**

This scripture may seem to be very simple at first glance but it is not simple in its application to our lives. Are you placing God as your first priority in your life? Are you loving Him and serving Him with your whole heart? What other priorities take precedence over Him?

I encourage you to re-prioritize your life to the Lord with Him having first place in your life.

Love the Lord with all your heart. He loves you and He's got you. Trust Him to guide you and reward you for diligently seeking after Him.

Jennifer

Prayer Request

November 17

> "Do what is right and good in the Lord's sight so that it will go well with you and you may go in and take over the good land the Lord promised on oath to your ancestors."
>
> **DEUTERONOMY 6:18**

Are you the person in your family or in your circle of friends who always tries to "do the right thing" when faced with a dilemma? Do people turn to you when they are seeking answers to difficult situations? If so, consider yourself blessed. You are setting an example of integrity. Humbly submit yourself to the wisdom and authority of the Lord and He will guide you.

Do what is right always and in every situation. Even when it seems unfair. Even when it hurts. Even when others don't understand what you're doing, always do what is RIGHT. The Lord sees you and He will reward you.

Jennifer

Prayer Request

November 18

> "As God's partners, we beg you not to accept this marvelous gift of God's kindness and then ignore it. For God says, 'At just the right time, I heard you. On the day of salvation, I helped you.' Indeed, the "right time" is now. Today is the day of salvation."
>
> **2 CORINTHIANS 1:2**

Did you know that you are a partner with Christ? When you believe in Him, you are called to spread His love, compassion, mercy, and THE GOOD NEWS of salvation! It is good news indeed!

1. Don't ignore what God has done for you. Tell others!
2. Don't ignore the people He places in your life. Love them!
3. Don't ignore the blessings in your life. Thank God!

Jennifer

Prayer Request

November 19

"For God did not give us a spirit of fear, but
a spirit of power, love, and self-discipline."

2 TIMOTHY 1:7

Whom or What makes you fearful? What is your response to those people or situations that cause you fear?

As believers, we have been given a spirit of POWER, love, and self-discipline. Speak this verse of 2 Timothy 1:7 over yourself and let it sink into the core of your being as you become courageous every day. Your mind will be renewed by speaking words of life, not fear.

Do NOT fear. He is with you.

Jennifer

Prayer Request

....

....

November 20

"Without wood a fire goes out; without
a gossip a quarrel dies down."

PROVERBS 26:20

We have all heard the childish saying, "Sticks and stones may hurt my bones, but words will never hurt me." How completely untrue! Gossip can be very destructive to someone's character, which can negatively impact their families, their careers, and their future endeavors.

Words can hurt and words can heal. Use your words for character building, encouraging, and expressing God's love to others. You may regret speaking harshly to someone, but you will never regret speaking kind words. Use uplifting words to encourage someone on this lifetime journey we are traveling together!

Jennifer

Prayer Request

November 21

> "Trust in the Lord with all of your heart and lean not on your own understanding. In all your ways acknowledge Him and He will direct your paths."
>
> **PROVERBS 3:5-6**

Do you need direction? Do you need clarity about a particular situation?

In ALL of your ways acknowledge the Lord and watch Him direct your paths. He is working on your behalf at all times. He loves you and He has a plan for your life. Trust Him as He will direct your paths when you humbly acknowledge Him as the Lord of your life.

Jennifer

Prayer Request

November 22

> "And I will give you a new heart and I put a new spirit in you. I will take out your stony, stubborn heart and give you a tender, responsive heart."
>
> **EZEKIEL 36:26**

Do you need a "heart transplant" today? Check yourself and ask if ALL of your thoughts towards others motivated by love? Do your own selfish ambitions, goals, or desires come into play in your interactions with others? Are you truly motivated by love? Do you harbor hate, resentment, or unforgiveness towards others?

Be real with yourself and ask the question honestly: Do. You. Need. A. New. Heart? A heart that lives to please God above all else. Ask Him to help you with a "heart transplant" today. It's not too late and you're not too old.

Let Him replace your heart with His perfect, pure, and wonderful love in your heart.

Jennifer

Prayer Request

November 23

"Do not fret because of those who are evil or be envious of those who do wrong; for like the grass, they will soon wither, like green plants, they will soon die away."

PSALM 37: 1-2

Do you ever look around you and wonder why everyone else seems to be moving forward at a faster pace than you?

Do you know people who are dishonest, untrustworthy, or corrupt in their business dealings yet they still appear to be prosperous? Friend, quit looking around, quit comparing, quit fretting, and look up!

God's got you. There is nothing too difficult for Him. Seek Him first and He will guide you on the best path for your life.

Again, quit looking around and look UP!

Jennifer

Prayer Request

November 24

> "Speak up for those who cannot speak for themselves, for the rights of all who are destitute. Speak up and judge fairly; defend the rights of the poor and needy."
>
> **PROVERBS 31: 8-9**

Do you advocate for others? Do you speak for those cannot speak for themselves? Are you compassionate towards others, seeking to assist them as needed?

I truly believe that most people have a genuine desire to help others. Most people also have the best of intentions in rendering assistance to those less fortunate; however, they allow other situations to prevent them from actually following through with those good intentions, such as procrastination, perfectionism, or greed.

This life on earth is temporary and every day is one day closer to eternity. Make your time on this earth as productive and fruitful as possible. Dedicate your life to the Lord and watch how He will help you make a difference in the lives of others.

If you want to experience true happiness, serve others!

Jennifer

Prayer Request

November 25

> "Brothers and sisters, we urge you to warn those who are lazy. Encourage those who are timid. Take tender care of those who are weak. Be patient with everyone."
>
> **1 THESSALONIANS 5:14**

As we begin this week of Thanksgiving, I encourage each one of us to read that scripture verse again. When Paul wrote this letter to the church in Thessalonica, he was providing advice and direction to a new group of believers. As believers, we are called to encourage, edify, take care of each other and not be lazy.

How does this specific verse apply to us today? First of all, we need to realize that we have a limited time on this earth. Each day matters and your time is a valuable resource. Use it wisely. Work hard at whatever God has called you to do with your life!

If you're married, love your spouse wholeheartedly. If you're a parent, love and encourage your children. If you're employed, work as for the Lord rather than people. If you are blessed to be surrounded by friends and family, love them and cherish them. If you have financial wealth, be a good steward of it. If you have a home, take care of it. If you have a useful skill or trade, use it for the Lord. And don't keep your salvation a secret....SHARE THE GOOD NEWS with others!

When you are focused on your eternal life, your daily perspective will radically change for the better!

Jennifer

Prayer Request

November 26

"Everyone was gripped with great wonder and awe, and they PRAISED God, exclaiming, 'We have seen amazing things today!"

LUKE 5:26

Jesus performed miracles while He was on the earth, which amazed a majority of the people and in some situations, these miracles provoked doubt. Yet despite all of the miracles that He performed and all the GOOD that He did during His life on earth, there were still people who doubted that He was truly the Son of God.

He loved everyone, everywhere, in every circumstance. And He still does today.

Friend, you don't need a miracle to know these simple facts: He loves you, He is for you, He wants good for you, and He wants a relationship with you. You are the miracle and you can also become a miracle for someone else. Go put some kindness into the world today. Speak hope, love and faith!

Jennifer

Prayer Request

November 27

> "Because He turned His ear toward me, I will pray as long as I live!"
>
> **PSALM 116:2**

As we enter into the Thanksgiving holidays, we all feel compelled to reach out to loved ones to check in with them, make dinner plans, and coordinate schedules for spending time together. Everyone wants to hear from their loved ones during the busy holiday season. But did you know that the Lord also wants to hear from you?

Just as if we are calling our parents, our children, or our friends, make time to "call out" to the Lord this Thanksgiving season. Praise Him for everything He has done in your life. Thank Him for being your very best friend. Let Him know ALL the details of your life: the good, the bad, and the ugly details. He can handle it. He cares and He listens to you.

Much love and blessing to you!

Jennifer

Prayer Request

. . . .

. . . .

November 28

"Give freely and become more wealthy,
be stingy and lose everything."

PROVERBS 11:24

When was the last time you donated something in new or good condition? More often that not, it is easier to donate old, rejected, broken, or dirty items to an organization rather than donating new or gently used items that are clean, repaired, and in good working condition.

The Thanksgiving season is an opportunity to express our gratitude. As you spend time with family and friends, be genuinely grateful for the time you have with each one of them. And as the table is cleared and the Thanksgiving season is officially completed, take a minute to look around your home.

What items do you see around you that you can give to someone else? Furniture, clothing, kitchen items? As you begin to locate those items, clean them, wash them, repair them, and then donate them! You've also just cleared some free space in your home to begin transitioning into the Christmas season.

Be GENEROUS this season. Donate items, share your home with good company, and love the people whom the Lord places in your path. Remember, it is a journey homeward for us all.

Jennifer

Prayer Request

November 29

"Pour out your unfailing love on those who love You; give justice to those with honest hearts."

PSALM 36:10

Our prayers go up to heaven but are they answered the exact way we want them to be answered? How many times have you prayed for a specific situation and you felt like God wasn't listening or didn't care?

Friend, know this: He hears you and He loves you with a steadfast, unfailing, and never-ending love! Keep seeking His face and His will for your life. When you pray for your heart to be aligned with His will, you may determine that your prayer request changes as you draw closer to Him. He will guide you and transform your life.

Jennifer

Prayer Request

November 30

"And may you have the power to understand, as all God's people should, how wide, how long, how high, and how deep His love is."

EPHESIANS 3:18

Have you ever tried to swim laps in a large pool? As an adolescent, I was on the swim team and I still remember the exhaustion of swimming multiple laps while being timed for a speed. There were times that I thought the long pool lap lanes were truly endless.

When I read this scripture, I think about the magnitude of an ocean in contrast to a pool. If I thought an Olympic size pool was endless, then imagine trying to swim the entire ocean. How wide, how long, and how deep are our oceans?

In contrast, our oceans are considered the "next frontier" for scientific discoveries. Our oceans are vast and significantly unexplored. The exact depths and widths of our oceans, to include the identification of every species of aquatic life, is still under discovery.

When God says He loves us, He means it. We cannot imagine how deep, how wide, or how long that unconditional love truly is! He LOVES you, friend, and He means what He says about the magnitude of His love for you.

Jennifer

Prayer Request

DECEMBER

"Now, a person who is put in charge as a manager must be faithful."

1 Corinthians 4:2

December 1

"Now, a person who is put in charge
as a manager must be faithful."

1 CORINTHIANS 4:2

Do you have responsibilities at your place of employment? What about in your home? Are you the person who manages finances, service contracts, clients, or employees? Are you a parent? Do you help with your own elderly parents? Do you serve on boards for civic organizations? Volunteer at your church?

Whatever your responsibilities are, do them to the best of your ability. Does this mean that you have to be "perfect" all the time? Absolutely not because we aren't perfect! But please don't use our human imperfection as an excuse to not challenge yourself to rise higher in every area of your life.

Be excellent! Trust the Lord to show you the areas for improvement in your life and He will lead you through the process of refinement. Trust Him.

Jennifer

Prayer Request

....

....

December 2

"Oh, how my soul praises the Lord. How my spirit rejoices in God my Savior! For He took notice of his lowly servant girl, and from now on all generations will call me blessed. For the Mighty One is holy, and He has done great things for me. He shows mercy from generation to generation to all who fear Him."

LUKE 1: 46-50

Mary's song of praise shows us that she knew who she was: the chosen one to carry the Messiah in her womb. What an honor but yet what a responsibility! She was young and unmarried. She was a simple servant girl who genuinely loved God and wanted to be obedient to His calling on her life.

During Christmas and Easter seasons, let's remember WHOM we are celebrating...JESUS. What can you do to honor Him every Christmas season? You can show His love, His compassion, His mercy, His forgiveness, His generosity, and His unfailing grace to others during the Christmas season and every day on this earth.

Blessings to you and your family,

Jennifer

Prayer Request

December 3

> "A hot-tempered person stirs up a conflict; but the one who is patient calms a quarrel."
>
> **PROVERBS 15:18**

How many times have you heard that patience is a virtue? Why do you think patience is so highly valued among believers?

Upon reflection, whatever initially appears to the issue in an argument typically is actually just a "symptom" of whatever is truly going on with them. The next time that a heated argument occurs between you and someone else, I challenge you to pause, take a breath, and try to see their perspective. Discuss the matter after you've had time to pray about it. Exercise your patience.

Not every single situation we encounter is a burning fire emergency so don't ignite it! Your patience will be a reward for yourself and others when you develop it through exercising it.

Jennifer

Prayer Request

....

....

December 4

"Trust in the Lord with all your heart and do not depend on your own understanding. Seek His will in all you do, and He will show you which path to take."

PROVERBS 3:5-6

Have you ever walked on a path outside at night using a flashlight as your guide? Most likely the flashlight illuminated your next step on the path and your feet moved in that direction.

In a similar way, we should rely on the Lord to direct our path of life. The "flashlight" is anything (such as reading the Bible, prayer, Godly counsel from others) that guides on His path for our lives.

When you earnestly seek Him in all you do, He will direct you. Use the Light to reflect His goodness, mercy, and grace to others.

Jennifer

Prayer Request

December 5

"So then faith comes by hearing and hearing by the word of God."

ROMANS 10:17

What is faith? The dictionary definition of faith is "complete trust and confidence in someone or something."

Complete trust. Complete confidence. Pause a minute and re-read that definition of faith.

Whatever situation you're facing, give it to the Lord. Pray to Him, listen to His guiding, and increase your faith as you completely trust Him. Walking with Him as you travel through the peaks and valleys of life will bring a sense of peace that passes all human understanding.

Jennifer

Prayer Request

December 6

"He gives power to the weak and strength to the powerless."

ISAIAH 40:29

It's the beginning of December and already the "season" has begun: socials, parties, lunches, dinners, events, volunteer activities, family gatherings, shopping, cooking, exercising, wrapping presents, decorating, packing, and traveling. This may become overwhelming but I encourage you to slow down and enjoy the season.

There seems to be a constant struggle to do it all. Juggling work commitments and spending time with family and friends isn't an easy task! Children on school break further adds to the challenge of finding a balance. It can leave you feeling overwhelmed, powerless, and completely out of control.

When you start to feel overwhelmed, give it to God. Every single day I encourage you to submit your day and all of your plans to the Lord and ask Him to order your steps. He will give you the strength and true JOY you need in your life.

Jennifer

Prayer Request

December 7

> "We are confident of all of this because of our great trust in God through Christ. It is not that we think we are qualified to do anything on our own. Our qualification comes from God."
>
> **2 CORINTHIANS 3:4**

Are you trusting God with your life? Are you trusting Him with your entire life from start to completion? Yes, friend, we are instructed to trust God with our lives, here, now, and through eternity.

This is a reoccurring theme throughout the scriptures. For those of us who are planners and like to know what's ahead, this can become an ongoing struggle.

Here's what I know to be true in my own life: He loves me and He created me for a purpose. I am uniquely designed to run my own race, equipped with strength, talents, and natural abilities. What He started in me He will bring to completion. He is a good, good Father and He can be trusted with my heart's desires in all areas of my life. And if He did it for me, He can do it for you!

Jennifer

Prayer Request

December 8

> "The disciples were amazed. 'Who is this man?' they asked. 'Even the winds and waves obey him!'"
>
> **MATTHEW 8:27**

Boats don't sink because of the storm around them. Boats sink because of what gets into them. Are you allowing the storms of your life to get into your life boat?

With the help of Jesus, we can navigate through the storms of life by surrendering our life plans to His plans and allowing Him to calm the waves of uncertainty within us.

1. IN Him, there is peace.
2. IN Him, there is wisdom.
3. IN Him, there is clarity.
4. IN Him, there is love.
5. IN Him, there is humility.
6. IN Him, there is compassion and mercy.
7. IN Him, there is obedience and surrender.
8. IN Him, there is grace.

The wind and the waves obeyed Him because He was and still is the Lord. Ask HIM to come into your boat.

Jennifer

Prayer Request

December 9

> "Jesus turned around, and when He saw her He said, 'Daughter, be encouraged! Your faith has made you well.' And the woman was healed at that moment."
>
> **MATTHEW 9:22**

Friend, do you have situations in your life that need a touch from the Lord? My question to you is have you reached out to Him? He's always available 24 hours a day, 7 days a week, to listen to your prayers.

When we reach out to the Lord in faith, He responds with His healing power and wisdom. His strength will flow through you as you connect to Him in prayer. And your prayers don't have to eloquent. Your prayers only need to be sincere.

Go to Him and talk to Him today. He is always faithful, ever present, and completely dedicated to YOU!

Jennifer

Prayer Request

....

....

December 10

"Jesus asked him, 'What do you want me to do for you?' 'Lord, he said, ' I want to see!' And Jesus said, 'All right, receive your sight! Your faith has healed you!"

MARK 10:51-52

Why do you think that Jesus asked the man what he wanted Jesus to do for him?

Do you think that Jesus somehow didn't know what was wrong with the man?

I assert to you that Jesus knew exactly what was wrong (the man was blind) and Jesus wanted to know that the blind man had the faith to ask for what he needed.

Friend, combine some actions with your faith. Start moving in the direction that the Lord points you. The Lord loves you and wants to help you! He is a good, good Father!

JUST ASK HIM!

Jennifer

Prayer Request

December 11

"I lay down and slept, yet I woke up in safety,
for the Lord was watching over me."

PSALM 3:5

Are you able to peacefully sleep at night? Is anything weighing on your mind, possibly causing you to toss and turn?

Friend, I hear you! I also have some sleepless nights sometimes and I understand how tired you can be the day after a restless night. It is no fun to stay awake when you know your body needs rest.

May I suggest an alternative to you? If you're concerned over a particular matter, pray about it! If you have a medical condition preventing you from sleeping at night, make an appointment with your physician. There may be an underlying health condition that needs to be treated.

Are you eating healthy and exercising on a regular basis? Are you managing your daily activities though a time management/daily planner? Are you leaving electronic devices on in your bedroom? It may just be a simple change that needs to occur and then you'll start sleeping great again!

Instead of fretting about your lack of sleep, I encourage you to pray about it first, seek divine wisdom, and follow through on whatever behaviors you may need to change to positively affect your sleeping patterns.

Rest well!

Jennifer

Prayer Request

December 12

"Your word is a lamp to my feet and light to my path."

PSALM 119:105

I went hiking today and as I climbed a very large incline, I literally ran out of steam. The combination of consuming less calories, the elevation, and fact that I'd already been on the trail for hours finally took its toll. I sat down on a large red rock and just exhaled.

When we returned to the trail, I thought I heard the cry of a mountain lion echoing in the woods. Let me tell you, my energy quickly returned and I hustled over the rocky path with no problem! Yes, fear motivated me to move my feet but FAITH kept my sanity in the process. I prayed, sang, and whistled the entire time.

What is motivating you today? Faith or Fear? God does not give us a spirit of fear.

Is God asking you to move your feet in a certain direction? Is fear holding you back from obeying Him? Let His word (the Bible) light up your path of life! Listen to Him today. Surround yourself with praise and immerse yourself in the Bible.

Jennifer

Prayer Request

December 13

> I have seen what they do; but I will heal them anyway!
> I will lead them. I will comfort those who mourn, bringing
> praise to their lips. May they have abundant peace,
> both near and far, says the Lord who heals them."
>
> **ISAIAH 57:18-19**

What do you think pleases God? A heart that is sincere. Acts of kindness that are performed without any hidden agenda. Grace extended to those who don't deserve it. Mercy and forgiveness of others. Reaching out to those who need comfort. Encouraging others. Visiting the sick. Praying with others. Donating your time/talent/treasure/acts of service to your church.

What else can you think of that you can do that would please God?

I challenge you today to make this a day that you do your very best to please God. He loves us without limitations so why not at least try to please Him? It doesn't have to be anything elaborate to begin small acts of kindness so just do it.

Jennifer

Prayer Request

....

....

December 14

"Do not despise these small beginnings, for the Lord rejoices to see the work begin, to see the plumb line in Zerubbabel's hand."

ZECHARIAH 4:10

Do you have a dream in your heart to start a business? Maybe a dream to become a stay at home parent? Or a dream to be able to spend more time each day reading your favorite books? Or perhaps a dream to become physically fit? What about a dream to have a large savings account to protect against emergencies? Or a dream to have better relationships with your family and friends? A dream to successfully retire?

I encourage you to start TODAY! Start with small steps and stay faithful to the process. Pray, pray, pray, and start creating an action plan. Small beginnings are often the best way to reach your dreams!

Jennifer

Prayer Request

December 15

"And why do you worry about a speck in your friend's eye when you have a log in your own?"

LUKE 6:41

What are you dwelling on right now? Is there anything or anyone whom you are judging harshly? Anyone whom you believe you could easily critique their style, their habits, their behaviors, their past actions, or their attitudes?

Quit. Cease and desist. Refrain from the being the prosecutor, Judge, and jury for the trial/harsh criticism of another person.

Focus on changing your own behaviors before dwelling on someone else's behavior. Focus on bringing good into the world and loving others.

Jennifer

Prayer Request

December 16

> "Is there any encouragement from belonging to Christ? Any comfort from His love? Any fellowship together in the Spirit? Are your hearts tender and compassionate? Then make me truly happy by agreeing wholeheartedly with each other, loving one another, and working together with one mind and purpose."
>
> **PHILIPPIANS 2:1-2**

Please read those two (2) verses. Now read them again.

When Paul wrote this to the Philippians, he was attempting to encourage unity and harmony among believers. Wherever there is discord and strife, there is a sense of frustration in finding your purpose.

Paul's words are still applicable today. As believers, we are to work together, with a united purpose, placing others needs above our own, carrying one another's burdens, and encouraging one another to reach the finish line of this life.

Let your life be a life of purpose and let it be well-lived to your highest potential.

Jennifer

Prayer Request

December 17

> "Don't store up treasures here on earth, where moths eat them and rust destroys them and where thieves break in and steal. Store your treasures in heaven, where moths and rust cannot destroy, and thieves do no break in and steal. Wherever your treasure is, there the desires of your heart will also be."
>
> **MATTHEW 6: 19-21**

Do you have a favorite item that has been passed down throughout your family line? For example, it may be a piece of china, an old photograph, or perhaps a lovely necklace. Think about whatever the item is and then answer this question: It would be safe to say that particular item is truly treasured, wouldn't it?

Just as we cherish items that have been handed down through our generations, we should treasure the gift of our Salvation. When we accepted Christ in our hearts, we became a Believer. And as a believer, we are called to witness to others, tithe to our church, cherish our loved ones, encourage others, be merciful and kind, pray for others, and show compassion to all. Every time we do these acts of service in love, we are making "deposits" into our heavenly bank account.

May you be exceedingly wealthy in heavenly places!

Jennifer

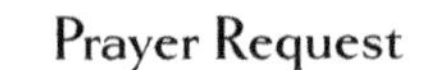

Prayer Request

....

....

December 18

> "But when you pray, go away by yourself, shut the door behind you, and pray to your Father in private. Then your Father who sees everything will reward you."
>
> **MATTHEW 6:6**

When you have a conversation with someone with whom you are in close relationship, you typically don't broadcast your conversations to others. Whether you communicate via text, phone, Facetime, email, or face-to-face, I feel certain there are come conversations that you have with some people that are always conducted in private. Genuine, heartfelt prayer is like having a conversation with the Lord.

Prayer doesn't have to be anything elaborate or eloquent. Come as you are, right here and right now, lifting our concerns to the throne of Grace. He listens, He cares, and He is trustworthy. He is the best and most loyal friend you will ever have in your entire life.

Wherever you are in life and whatever situations you're dealing with, know that you can TRUST Him with your heart! Start by having a relationship with Him.

Jennifer

Prayer Request

December 19

"For You are great and perform wonderful deeds. You alone are God. Teach me Your ways, O Lord, that I may live according to Your truth! Grant me purity of heart, so that I may honor You. With all my heart I will praise You, O Lord my God. I will give glory to Your name forever."

PSALM 86: 11-12

You are the hands and feet of Jesus on this earth. If you see someone in need, help them. If you see someone who needs encouragement, open your mouth and speak encouraging words to them. If you see someone who needs financial assistance, assist them until they are able to assist themselves. If you see someone who is lonely, call, write, or visit them.

If you know of someone who is sick, pray for them, visit them, go grocery shopping for them, or perhaps drive them to their physician's appointments. It doesn't have to be a grandiose event for you to help someone in need.

Start small if you need to but don't wait a minute longer because you need to just start today! BE THE HANDS AND FEET OF JESUS ON THIS EARTH!

Jennifer

Prayer Request

December 20

"Dry bones, listen to the word of the Lord! this is what the Sovereign Lord says: Look! I am going to put breath into you and make you live again! I will put flesh on you and cover you with skin. I will put breath into you and you will come to life. Then you will know that I am the Lord." Ezekiel 37:4-6

This vision that occurred to Ezekiel in a dream is prophetic in that spiritually dead people would be brought back to life again from hearing the Word of God. That same vision holds true today.

What "deadness" do you have in your spiritual life? Do you have a relationship with the Lord? Ask Him into your heart and believe that He Is Who He Says He Is. He loves you. He is for you, not against you. He wants you to have a future and a hope. He has a purpose for you. You are not a mistake. You are the apple of His eye and you are chosen by Him.

Friend, I pray that every "dead" situation in your life becomes rejuvenated with the love of the Lord. When Jesus Christ enters into your heart, you have abundant life. As a Christian believer, please know that this earth is not the end of the road for you and it is not your final destination. There is so much more than what this world can offer you when you believe in the Lord!

Jennifer

Prayer Request

December 21

> "When someone has been given much, much will be required in return; and when someone has been entrusted with much, even more will be required."
>
> **LUKE 12:48**

What has the Lord given you? Examples are Health, Talents, Ability to Earn an Income, or Educational Opportunities? I challenge you to fully develop each one of your God-given talents, skills, and abilities.

Don't waste a minute in becoming whom God has called you to be on this earth. Be diligent, productive, and faithful to Him and His calling on your life.

What or whom has the Lord ENTRUSTED to you? Your spouse, your children, your parents, your friends, your co-workers, your family? Nurture, protect, and develop the relationships that the Lord has entrusted into your care.

Jennifer

Prayer Request

December 22

"The next day John saw Jesus coming toward him and said, 'Look, the Lamb of God, who takes away the sin of the world!'"

JOHN 1:29

As we prepare for Christmas, I encourage you to take some time to reflect on all of your blessings. It is very easy to dwell on what we don't have, as opposed to what we do actually have as believers in Jesus Christ. Start counting your blessings, beginning with your salvation.

We celebrate Christmas as the birth of the Messiah and exchange gifts in remembrance of the gifts that the Wise Men brought to Him. We are acknowledging that HE is the Lord of ALL!

Jennifer

Prayer Request

December 23

"Then you will experience God's peace, which exceeds anything we can understand. His peace will guard your hearts and minds as you live in Christ Jesus."

PHILIPPIANS 4:7

I encourage you to take a moment today to read Paul's letter to the Philippians. If you don't have much time to read, start with Chapter 4. It is so relevant to our hectic, fast-paced society and lifestyle today.

In verse 4, we are encouraged to always be full of joy. In verse 5, we are instructed to be considerate in everything that we do. In verse 6, we are told to not worry about anything but pray about everything. We are further advised that we should thank Him for all He has done for us.

In this Christmas season, it is easy to focus on completing our "To Do" lists, participate in the mall shopping frenzy, and have baking adventures in the kitchen. I encourage you to slow down!

Pray, THANK GOD for what He's done in your life, worry less, and experience God's incredible peace. Be blessed!

Jennifer

Prayer Request

December 24

"Therefore, God elevated Him to the place of highest honor and gave Him the name above all other names, that at the name of Jesus every knee should bow, in heaven and on earth and under the earth, and every tongue confess that Jesus Christ is Lord, to the glory of God the Father."

PHILIPPIANS 2:9-11

Merry Christmas Eve! In the hustle and bustle of last minute preparations I am continually reminding myself that tomorrow is Christmas and tomorrow is the birthday celebration for Jesus!

Don't you just love our God? He's always doing things His unique way! The Son of God could have been born anywhere but God chose the most humble location. Jesus was born in a simple manger but yet wise men traveled from great distances to pay homage to Him.

He died on a cross among a cruel and disbelieving crowd. And then, if that incredible sacrifice wasn't enough, He rose from the grave and astonished everyone. And He still lives today! Invite Him into your heart this Christmas.

When you celebrate Christmas this year, remember that He had to be born in order to die. And He had to die in order to save us from our sins. So that's what we are celebrating: JESUS is LORD of ALL! #wehaveanawesomeGod

Jennifer

Prayer Request

December 25

> "Whatever is good and perfect comes down to us from God our Father, who created all the lights in the heavens.
>
> **JAMES 1:17**

Thank you, Lord, for the BEST GIFT of Your precious Son!

When we celebrate Christmas, it isn't simply about opening presents or overindulging in desserts. While a celebration is certainly appropriate, it is important to remember WHOM we are celebrating and why we are celebrating His birth. The birth of our Savior is a celebration that we need to enjoy every year.

Merry CHRISTmas!

Jennifer

Prayer Request

....

....

December 26

> "Understand this, my dear brothers and sisters. You must all be quick to listen, slow to speak, and slow to get angry. Human anger does not produce the righteousness God desires. So get rid of all the filth and evil in your lives and humbly accept the word of God has planted in your hearts, for it has the power to save your souls."
>
> **JAMES 1:19-21**

Wow! That scripture is a zinger! For me, it has been very convicting!

How often do we believe that our anger is justified? How frequently do we jump to conclusions?

For example, when was the last time you finished someone else's sentence for them? When you listen to someone talk, are you already crafting your response before they ever finish their sentence?

Re-read the scripture verse slowly. Allow it to resonate with you. Re-read it again. Apply it to your everyday life and watch your life be transformed.

Jennifer

Prayer Request

December 27

"What do you mean, 'If I can?" Jesus asked.
Anything is possible if a person believes."

MARK 9:23

Jesus is a healer. What physical, mental, emotional, financial or spiritual needs do you have in your life? Have you ASKED Jesus to help you, to guide you to the right physicians or medical treatment facility, and to give you strength and wisdom in how to treat disease? Have you asked Him to point you in the direction of a new career and are you willing to do what He asks of you? It could mean that that you sacrifice time and energy to return to school or to work two jobs to pay off debt.

Yes, Jesus can heal in a single second but sometimes He uses people, medicines, or discipline as the vessels or method for healing. Sometimes it is a radical healing and sometimes it is a slow process. He is God and His timing is perfect.

I pray right now that anyone reading this will ask the Lord for His wisdom and direction for whatever ails you. He CAN and He will help you if you would simply ASK Him! Nothing, nothing, nothing is impossible for our God.

Jennifer

Prayer Request

December 28

"The One who is in you is greater than
the one who is in the world."

1 JOHN 4:46

Whatever challenge or obstacle you are facing today is no match for our Lord. He is with you and He will sustain you.

When you accepted Him into your heart, you tapped into the true source of strength: JESUS!

1. Need a listening ear? He's there.
2. Need wisdom? He's there. He will sustain you, friend, I promise you!
3. Need encouragement? He can do it.
4. Need love? He does love you!

Call out to Him, seek Him in His word, pray for wisdom and discernment in all situations in your life. And get ready and be expectant that He will do what He says He will do!

Jennifer

Prayer Request

December 29

"But for you who fear my name, the Sun of Righteousness will rise with healing in His wings. And you will go free, leaping with joy likes calves let out to pasture."

MALACHI 4:2-3

I recently completed reading a book by TD Jakes entitled, "When Women Pray", and he referenced this scripture verse as it relates to praying for salvation and experiencing the pure joy that comes from being rescued. I encourage each one of us to examine our lives where we feel pressured or enslaved to old habits, concerns, negative thoughts or behaviors. Invite the Lord into your situation and allow Him to be present in all areas of your life. Don't put the Lord in a box!

Friend, I pray that whatever is burdening you, weighing you down, or causing you to feel distress, is removed from you. May you end this year dancing and leaping like a calf, knowing that your true JOY comes from the Lord.

Jennifer

Prayer Request

December 30

"Seek the Kingdom of God above all else and
He will give you everything you need."

LUKE 12: 31

Do you have everything that you need? Are you lacking in a certain area? Have you prayed about it? Have you sought Godly counsel on the matter? Are you taking steps towards the solution or are you sitting idle, waiting on God to do it all for you?

Yes, God can do the impossible! Yet not doing what you can with what you have is to ignore the gifts and talents He already placed inside of you. Develop those gifts, nurture those strengths, seek assistance for areas of growth, and remain focused on the path that He has created for you.

You have a divine purpose. You have unique skills and talents. Water those seeds planted inside of you and watch what happens!

Jennifer

Prayer Request

December 31

> "What a wildly wonderful world, God! You made it all, with Wisdom at Your side, made the earth overflow with Your wonderful creations."
>
> **PSALM 104:24**

He made the delicate wings of a butterfly and the tough hide of the elephant. He crafted the deep valleys in Grand Canyon and perfectly placed the stars in the sky. When you see a sunrise, know that it was the Lord who caused the new day to begin.

Enjoy this last day of the year and thank God for what He's done in your life this year and what He will continue to do in the next year. He is sovereign and He is Lord. What He started in you, He will bring to completion.

Take a moment today to look around you. These are little "gifts" of joy He has placed in nature for you to see His imagination and creativity. And then look at another magnificent creation: YOU!!

Be blessed, friends.

Jennifer

Prayer Request

....

....